Earnings Management and Its Determinants: Closing Gaps in Empirical Accounting Research

European University Studies
Europäische Hochschulschriften
Publications Universitaires Européennes

Series V
Economics and Management

Reihe V Série V
Volks- und Betriebswirtschaft
Sciences économiques, gestion d'entreprise

Vol./Bd. 3167

PETER LANG
Frankfurt am Main · Berlin · Bern · Bruxelles · New York · Oxford · Wien

Igor Goncharov

Earnings Management and Its Determinants: Closing Gaps in Empirical Accounting Research

PETER LANG
Europäischer Verlag der Wissenschaften

Bibliographic Information published by Die Deutsche Bibliothek
Die Deutsche Bibliothek lists this publication in the Deutsche Nationalbibliografie; detailed bibliographic data is available in the internet at <http://dnb.ddb.de>.

Zugl.: Bremen, Univ., Diss., 2005

D 46
ISSN 0531-7339
ISBN 3-631-54577-0
US-ISBN 0-8204-9807-6

www.peterlang.de

"Deiner heiligen Zeichen, o Wahrheit,
hat der Betrug sich angemaßt."

["All thy holy symbols, o truth,
deceit has adopted"]

Johann Christoph Friedrich von Schiller

Foreword

The current study is based on the PhD thesis I wrote during the time I worked as research assistant at the University of Bremen (Germany). The topic under analysis – earnings management – gained much attention in the academic literature in the 1990ies. The wave of high-profile company bankruptcies all over the world in the beginning of the XXI century escalated the problem and made its discussion public. As a result, the reputation for integrity and independence of the accounting profession and the confidence in financial statements were seriously damaged. I recall a cartoon picture in the newspaper portraying two prisoners: an old man wearing glasses and a younger man dressed in a t-shirt with an anarchy sign on it. The old man turns to the young man saying: "If you really want to smash capitalism, become an accountant". Practically, such an apocalyptic scenario is unlikely to occur, even if severe earnings manipulations may lead – at least under a theoretical perspective – to the collapse of capital markets. Nevertheless as earnings management is likely to persist in the future (at least as long as the incentives to manipulate earnings are present), causing damage to some stakeholders, it is important to understand why and when any wrongdoing occurs.

The current study contributes to a better understanding of earnings management. I would like to thank particularly the following persons for helping me during the work on the study. I am grateful for the advice and encouragement to my PhD supervisor Prof. Dr. Jochen Zimmermann (University of Bremen). I also express special thanks to Prof. Dr. Matthias Schmidt (University of Leipzig) for being the second referee and a member of the dissertation committee. Parts of the study have gained from the helpful comments of Dr. Dmitrij Volkov (St. Petersburg State University).

I thank Jens Schütte and Jörg-Richard Werner, who shared the office with me during the time I was working on the PhD thesis. I am particularly grateful to Jörg for suggested improvements and the comprehensive review of the thesis. Jens, thanks for the helpful pessimism and extensive personal discussions.

Finally, I must acknowledge the debt I owe to my parents. Their help and encouragement were crucial for the successful completion of my PhD thesis.

CONTENTS

CONTENTS

TABLE OF FIGURES

List of Tables

LIST OF SYMBOLS AND ABBREVIATIONS

A	total assets
a, b	predicted values of current (α) and non-current (β) weights respectively
$a_1, a_2, a_3, \ldots, a_n$	estimates of firm specific or group specific parameters
AA	accounting (i.e. total or aggregated) accruals
AAB	balance of noncash current assets (net of tax receivables) less current liabilities (net of tax payables) and depreciation and amortization expense
AccSt	dummy variable taking a value of one if company reports under U.S. GAAP and zero if a company reports either under German GAAP or IAS
ACFE	Association of Certified Fraud Examiners
AG	*Aktien Gesellschaft* (joint-stock company)
AICPA	American Institute of Certified Public Accountants
ASI	income from asset sales per share
Auto	the proportion of premiums earned in the low risk, short-tailed coverage lines of business
BDE	bad debt expense
BgBl	beginning balance allowance for bad debts
Cap	a dummy variable taking a value of 1 if the ratio of statutory surplus to net premiums earned is in the lowest quartile of the sample that year and 0 otherwise
CAPEX	capital expenditure
CCA	current component of total accruals, i.e. ΔWC
CFO	operating cash flows
CFOP	cash flow from operations computed as operating income less changes in working capital

cm	the gross cash contribution
CO	net charge-offs
COGS	cost of finished goods sold (including asset write-downs)
CP	cash paid to suppliers
CR	cash received from customers
DA	discretionary accruals
DAP	proxy for discretionary accruals (DAP) that measures accruals with error η
DASI	income from asset sales per share
DAX	*Deutscher Aktienindex* (German Stock Index)
DEP	current period depreciation and amortization expense
DETEQ	ratio of the book value of long-term debt to the book value of owners' equity
DRD	discretionary research and development expenditure
DREVIS	(discretionary) reserve revision
E	reported earnings
EΔNPL	expected change in non-performing loans
EBT	earnings before taxes
EM	earnings management indicator variable, taking the value of 1 if the firm's earnings observation is in the first positive interval and 0 for all other intervals to the right of zero
EndBl	ending balance provision for bad debts
EXP	all expenses other than depreciation expense
FASB	Financial Accounting Standards Board
FN	financing needs, measured as actual average rate of revenue growth per year from the year the company applied the new reporting standard until 2002

g	growth rate of research and development expenditure
GAAP	Generally Accepted Accounting Principles
Gr_REV	revenues growth from the current period to the next period scaled by the current period revenues
h	optimal bin width
HGB	*Handelsgesetzbuch* (German Commercial Code)
i	subscript denoting firm i
IAS	International Accounting Standards
IASB	International Accounting Standards Board
IFRS	International Financial Reporting Standards
Ind_j	a set of dummy variables representing first-digit SIC code industry groups
IPO	Initial Public Offering
IQR	interquartile range
k	slope coefficient that captures expected change in accounts receivable for one unit change in revenues
Lev	leverage, measured as the ratio of debt to total assets
LLA	the beginning balance in the loan loss allowance account
$Loans_j$	beginning balances of loans in six categories as a percentage of total loans: commercial and industrial loans, loans secured by real estate, loans to depositary institutions, loans to finance agricultural production, loans to foreign governments, loans to individuals
$LOut_j$	beginning balances of loans in six categories: commercial, consumer, real estate, foreign, loans to other financial institutions, and other loans
LTail	the proportion of premiums earned in the high risk, long-tailed coverage lines of business
MBO	management buyout

MDAX	*Mid Cap Deutscher Aktienindex* (German Mid Cap Stock Index)
med(…)	the median value
MTR	marginal tax rate, a binary variable equalling 1 if the firm's marginal tax rate is equal or higher than the top statutory tax rate and 0 otherwise
N	number of observations
n_a	actual number of observations in the interval
NAEST	an estimate of nondiscretionary accruals
NCCA	non-current component of total accruals, i.e. Dep
NCF	net cash flows or change in the cash account
NDA	nondiscretionary accruals
NDCCA	nondiscretionary current component of total accruals
NDCFO	nondiscretionary operating cash flows
NDCOGS	nondiscretionary costs of goods sold
NDExp	nondiscretionary mandatory expenditure: a sum of nondiscretionary research and development, advertising and selling, general and administrative expenses
NDLCO	nondiscretionary loan charge-offs
NDLLA	nondiscretionary loan loss allowance
NDLLP	nondiscretionary loan loss provision
NDNCCA	nondiscretionary non-current component of total accruals
NDProd	nondiscretionary production costs
NDPROV	nondiscretionary provision for bad debts
NDRSGL	nondiscretionary realized security gains and losses scaled by lagged total assets
NDΔInv	nondiscretionary changes in inventory
n_e	expected number of observations in the interval

NEMAX	*Neuer Markt Aktienindex* (New Market Stock Index)
NOL_{τ}	a dummy variable taking a value of 1 if firm has net operating loss carryforwards and 0 otherwise
OAO	*Otkrytoe Akcionernoe Obshchestvo* (open joint-stock company)
OCAL	other current assets and liabilities
OLS	Ordinary Least Squares
OOO	*Obshchestvo s Ogranichennoj Otvetstvennost'yu* (limited liability company)
p	1, 2, ..., P is a firm subscript indicating firms for which earnings are predicted to be managed upwards
P	contemporaneous stock price performance
PPE	gross property, plant and equipment
Prod	production costs
PROV	provision for bad debts
PUBLIC	a dummy variable that takes values of one for public firms and zero for private firms
PUR	purchases of materials
q	1, 2, ..., Q is a firm subscript indicating firms for which earnings are predicted to be managed downwards.
Q1	first quartile
Q3	third quartile
R&D	research and development
R^2	coefficient of determination
RD	research and development expenditure
$RES_{\tau;\tau}$	loss reserve for year τ reported in the year τ
$RES_{\tau+5;\tau}$	the revised estimate of the year τ loss reserve reported in the year $\tau+5$

ROA	return on assets, measure as earnings deflated by total assets
SEC	Securities and Exchange Commission
SEO	Seasoned Equity Offering
SIC	Standard Industrial Classification
sm	the gross margin on sales
SR	smoothing ratio
t	a year subscript indicating a year in the estimation period
Tail	one minus the ratio of cash paid this year for prior year's business to loss reserves at the beginning of the year
UNGL	unrealized security gains and losses
UNIDEN	all no-cash current assets other then inventory and receivables and all current liabilities other than payables
U.S. GAAP	United States Generally Accepted Accounting Principles
Wkcomp	the proportion of premiums earned in the low risk, long-tailed coverage lines of business
WriteOffs	write-offs for the period
YEAR	a dummy variable equalling 1 for year 2002 and 0 for year 2001
z	test statistic approximately distributed under a Normal distribution
ZAO	*Zakrytoe Akcionernoe Obshchestvo* (closed joint-stock company)
$\alpha_1, \alpha_2, \alpha_3, \ldots, \alpha_n$	firm specific or group specific parameters
δ_1	prior year's receivables turnover $\frac{REC_{t-1}}{REV_{t-1}}$
δ_2	prior year's net current assets (less receivables and cash) turnover $\frac{OCAL_{t-1}}{EXP_{t-1}}$
δ_3	prior year's depreciation turnover $\frac{DEP_{t-1}}{PPE_{t-1}}$

ΔCA	change in current assets
ΔCash	change in cash and cash equivalents
ΔCL	change in current liabilities
ΔEPS	change in annual earnings per share before sales of assets and taxes
ΔINV	change in inventory
ΔNPL	the change in non-performing loans
ΔPAY	change in payables
ΔREC	change in net receivables
ΔREV	change in revenues
ΔSTD	change in debt included in current liabilities
ΔWC	change in working capital accruals
ζ	the residual revision
σ_E	standard deviation (σ) of earnings
σ_{NDE}	standard deviation (σ) of non-discretionary earnings (NDE)
ρ	correlation coefficient
τ	a year subscript indicating a year in the event period

1 INTRODUCTION

1.1 MOTIVATION FOR THE RESEARCH

The end of the 1990s and the beginning of the XXI century have witnessed a series of accounting scandals. The largest corporate bankruptcy in the United States – Enron in 2001 – was followed by a number of disclosures about errors in financial statements. Major Fortune 500 companies showed substantial accounting irregularities. Examples of these companies are Worldcom, AOL, Qwest Communications and Xerox. Accounting scandals were not restricted to the United States market. A number of European companies – Parmalat (Italy), Flowtex (Germany), Comroad (Germany), Royal Ahold (The Netherlands) – were also under the investigation of regulatory bodies. A total of 918 accounting-based securities litigation cases were filed for a period 1996 to 2003 in the U.S., from which 66 cases were against non-U.S. firms (PricewaterhouseCoopers, 2003a and 2003b). In the core of these scandals was usually earnings management, – a deliberate attempt to change the earnings figures to deceive some stakeholders. While the true amount of loss due to accounting scandals cannot be estimated, the accounting cases settlements for the period between 1996 and 2003 amount a total of 11,5 billion U.S. Dollars (PricewaterhouseCoopers, 2003a).

These scandals highlight the problem of optimal allocation of savings to investment opportunities. On one hand, households want to invest their savings. On the other hand there are a number of existing companies and new business offerings, which await households' savings. The allocation of savings to investments is complicated because of at least two reasons (Healy/Palepu, 2001): First, entrepreneurs usually have access to private information about the value of their business and an incentive to overstate this value. Such information asymmetries can result into the adverse selection of investment projects and in the worst case to a breakdown of the capital market (Akerlof, 1970). Second, once an investor has chosen a firm, an entrepreneur has an incentive to behave opportunistically and expropriate the investor's savings. Earnings management potentially contributes to these problems: The entrepreneur may overstate the value of a business by the means of earnings management to attract new investors. Once investors have invested their money, an entrepreneur may expropriate them, hiding such behaviour with earnings management. In both cases earnings management may distort the optimal allocation of savings to investment opportunities.

To resolve these problems and to improve the allocation of capital, it is necessary to understand the negative implications of earnings management and the situations in which earnings management occurs. The purpose of this analysis is twofold: to provide an overview of a research on earnings management determinants and to close some gaps in this field of accounting research. Determinants of earnings management are factors that influence the extent of earnings management. On one hand, these are the motivations to manage earnings. On the other hand, these are the factors that may constrain opportunistic behaviour. Knowing determinants of earnings management is crucial for remedying misallocations. First, if investors know conditions under which earnings management appears, they can either adjust the price for manipulations or invest their savings in another venture (e.g., to price securities with adjustment in those markets, where earnings management is widely spread). Second, if the regulatory bodies know motivations for earnings management, they can take more direct actions or at least re-think the strategy of selecting potential candidates for an inquiry (e.g., to take a closer look at firms that go public). Third, an effort can be undertaken to enforce the factors that constrain earnings management (e.g., strengthen the corporate governance norms).

To shed more light on the determinants of earnings management, it is, first, important to summarise the prior evidence of the research on motivations for and constraints of earnings management. An overview of results of empirical and theoretical papers will be provided to answer the following questions:

- What is earnings management and how it is related to earnings quality?
- How can earnings management be detected?
- What motivates companies to manage earnings? and
- What can constrain earnings management practices?

Research on motivations for and inhibitors of earnings management is manifold. Despite an intensive research in this field, several questions remain still unresolved. It is, for instance, unclear, whether accounting standards determine the level of earnings management and how different (competing) reporting incentives jointly determine the extent of earnings management. The following questions will be answered to close these existing research gaps:

- Can accounting standards influence the extent of earnings management?
- Is there an accounting framework that outperforms other in respect to the quality of earnings, prepared under this framework?
- What is the role of competing incentives in determining the extent of earnings management?
- Which incentives win and under which conditions?
- Is there earnings management for tax purposes in transformation economies? and
- Do the market forces determine the extent of earnings management?

These questions will be answered by means of an empirical analysis. Beyond providing additional evidence on the determinants of earnings management, results of the analysis will also have implications for the standard setters. German lawmakers and regulators have not yet taken a decision on which accounting standards should apply to non-listed companies in the future. They will probably choose between requiring the continued use of German Generally Accepted Accounting Principles (German GAAP) and allowing firms to move all reporting to IAS/IFRS. If the goal of these forthcoming regulatory decisions is to provide investors and other users of financial reports with reliable and informative data, lawmakers and regulators are likely to require companies to apply standards that reduce the levels of earnings management. The results of the analysis suggest that the move to IAS/IFRS is unlikely to increase the quality of financial reports.

One of the major purposes of the recent accounting reforms in Russia is the enforcement of high quality financial reporting that is transparent and useful for the stakeholders (and especially investors). Results of the analysis suggest that further reforms are necessary: Laws that will improve the functionality of the capital market and increase the tax enforcement are crucial to increase the quality of financial reports.

1.2 Structure of the Analysis

The further discussion is going to proceed as follows. The second chapter will give a definition of earnings management. To understand fully what comprises earnings management it is necessary to provide a critical overview of (empirical) earnings quality measures. Earnings management and earnings quality are often used interchangeably. While non-managed earnings imply an earnings measure of high quality, it will be shown that these two concepts are not identical. Earnings quality is a superordinate concept that incorporates earnings management. Earnings quality has a lot of empirical realisations (and therefore measures), some of which constitute earnings management; some are semi-strongly related to earnings management; and some are only hypothetically related to earnings management (i.e. a relation to earnings management is questionable). The other important point in the second chapter is the inclusion of certain instruments in the definition of earnings management.

The third chapter will give an overview of models used to detect earnings management. The main purpose of this chapter is to show the variety of techniques used to trace earnings management and to find the most suitable ones for the following empirical analyses. Different procedures may be used for detection of income manipulations. The chapter will discuss a group that is most suitable for academic research – statistical procedures. Statistical models are manifold.

The fourth chapter will summarise the results of the empirical research on the determinants of earnings management. On one hand, the motivations for earnings management will be analysed. On the other hand, it will be shown which factors constrain income manipulations. This overview is provided to identify gaps in empirical accounting research. Two subsequent sections of the chapter 4 will close some gaps. Two empirical questions are formulated and then tested on data samples from the German and the Russian markets: The first question is whether accounting standards matter, i.e. can accounting standards through the (amount of) provided accounting choices constrain earnings management behaviour. The second empirical analysis is mainly concerned with the role of competing incentives in explaining the extent of earnings management. This analysis builds on the foundations laid in chapters two and three. Chapter 5 will summarize the results of the analysis.

2 Earnings Management and the Quality of Earnings

2.1 Critical Review of Earnings Quality Concepts

2.1.1 Classification of Earnings Quality Concepts

Earnings numbers as indicators of firm performance are of tremendous importance for the users of financial statements. Different types of stakeholders are interested in their timely and accurate presentation. Examples include shareholders that assess managers' performance using earnings numbers, lenders that use earnings in debt covenant agreements to ensure the timely payment of debt and/or interest, customers that evaluate a continuing supply of product and related services, employees that assess the future prospects and the level of job security. A correct assessment of firm's performance depends to a large degree on the level of accounting information quality (or more specific – quality of earnings) provided to decision makers. This chapter will deal with issues related to the quality of earnings and will give an overview of existing earnings quality concepts and will relate them to earnings management. Sometimes the concepts of earnings management and earnings quality are used interchangeably, but it will be shown later that earnings quality is a broader concept that is only partly related to earnings management.

This chapter will discuss earnings quality concepts that can be empirically measured and were used in accounting research.[1] Certain earnings properties resulting from the application of GAAP cannot be measured empirically. Examples include comparability that is used in the conceptual framework of the International Accounting Standards Board (IASB) and of the Financial Accounting Standards Board (FASB), and understandability, which is a qualitative characteristic of accounting information according to the IASB's conceptual framework. Earnings quality concepts that do not lend themselves to empirical measures will be excluded from the scope of this chapter.[2]

Earnings quality is an abstract concept as quality cannot be directly observed. Current accounting research has not arrived at a consensus what exactly characterises "high quality" earnings. Most definitions are conceptually different from each other. They depend on certain properties of accounting earnings that are desirable outcomes of financial reporting from the view of e.g., researchers, standard setters, investors or ana-

---

1 Two empirical measures are out of the scope of this chapter: fraud accounting (e.g., Dechow et al. (1996) proxy with Securities and Exchange Commission (SEC) enforcement actions for the extreme low earnings quality) and suboptimal real cash flow decisions (e.g., opportunistic timing of asset sales discussed in Bartov (1993)). While these measures constitute both earnings quality and earnings management they will not be discussed in the section 2.1 for two reasons: First, these concepts were rarely (separately) used in accounting research. Second, they can be viewed as a part of earnings smoothing and loss avoidance.

2 The conceptual framework concepts that can be empirically measured (e.g., relevance and reliability) will be discussed in the subsequent sections.

lysts. As the desired outcomes are not necessarily related, the definitions and metrics of earnings quality vary. As there is no single definition of earnings quality it will be defined here depending on the perspective from which the quality is assessed. For example, from the perspective of economic income, sometimes referred to as „true income“, the representation of earnings quality is: "...the extent to which reported earnings faithfully represent Hicksian income..."[3] (Schipper/Vincent, 2003, p. 98). Low quality is in this case "...poor correspondence between observable accounting earnings and unobservable economic earnings..." (Bhattacharya et al., 2003, p. 642). However, from a valuation perspective: "...earnings [...] is of good quality if it is a good indicator of future earnings" (Penman/Zhang, 2002, p. 237). Then "...earnings that are more persistent are viewed as higher quality" (Richardson, 2003, p. 49).

Some of the earnings quality concepts can be viewed from several perspectives. As the latter vary the same earnings quality metric can indicate both: earnings of high and low quality. One example is earnings smoothing. Smoothed earnings (measured as e.g., correlation between accruals changes and operating cash flow changes) are a desired outcome of the accounting process from the valuation perspective (as smoothed earnings are considered to be of a high quality). From the perspective of economic income representation, however, smoothing deteriorates earnings quality.

Earnings quality concepts may be divided into two categories depending on the measure used. These are either market- or accounting-based measures (see Figure 1). Market-based measures are constructed using the association of market and accounting data (e.g., association of earnings and stock returns). These measures include: value relevance of earnings, timeliness in loss recognition/conservatism and earnings timeliness. Accounting-based measures are solely constructed with the help of data from companies' financial statements. Accounting-based measures include time-series properties of earnings, timeliness in loss recognition/conservatism, earnings smoothing, loss avoidance, accrual quality and the book-tax conformity.

The oldest concepts of earnings quality are earnings smoothing (e.g., Koch, 1981) and value relevance (e.g., Ball/Brown, 1968). Recent concepts include loss avoidance and timeliness of loss recognition/conservatism that could be related to the research of Hayn (1995) and Basu (1997) respectively. The next sections of the chapter will address the single earnings quality concepts in more detail and give an overview of empirical measures designed to assess the quality of earnings.

---

3 Hicksian income is defined as an amount that can be paid out as dividends during a period without affecting firm's prosperity (Hicks, 1939).

2.1.2 ACCOUNTING BASED MEASURES OF EARNINGS QUALITY

2.1.2.1 TIME-SERIES PROPERTIES OF EARNINGS

Two concepts will be reviewed in this section: earnings persistence and earnings predictability. These concepts are related to the distinct properties of time-series behaviour of earnings numbers.

Figure 1: Concepts of earnings quality

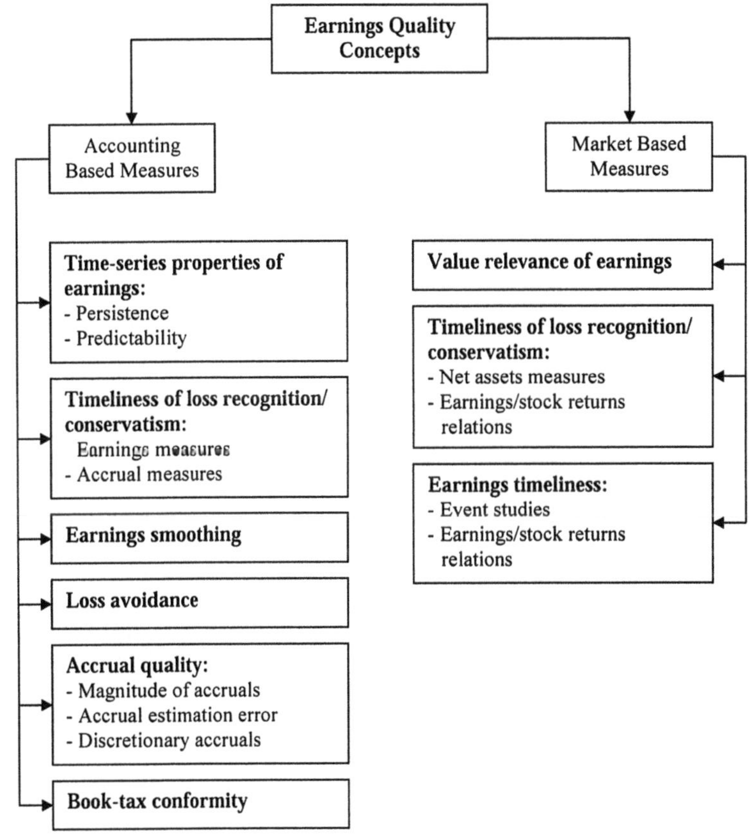

From the time-series perspective, earnings can be spited into two components: a permanent part (also referred to as sustainable or core earnings) and a transitory part. Permanent earnings are generated by business transactions that produce earnings innovations (or earnings shocks) that remain in future earnings realizations. Transitory components represent non-recurring items reported on the income statement (e.g., one time gains or losses from asset sales). Persistence and predictability relate to the time-series behaviour of earnings innovations. Persistence is defined as the extent to which current period innovations remain in the earnings series. Predictability is defined as "...the ability of past earnings to predict future earnings" (Lipe, 1990, p. 50) and is negatively related to the variance of innovations. Lipe (1990) gives several examples to illustrate the distinct properties of the two measures:

> "One can imagine a random walk and a white-noise series which have the same variance of shocks. The former has much more persistence, but the two are equally predictable (the forecast errors have the same variance). Alternatively, one can imagine two random-walk series with high and low variance of shocks, respectively. The former is less predictable, but the two have equal persistence." (Lipe, 1990, p. 52)

Persistence and predictability are desired outcomes of financial reporting from the valuation perspective. Earnings that are highly predictable and persistent are easier to predict. They can enter into valuation models without any adjustments (for e.g., non-recurring items). Both the theoretical and empirical literature show that persistent and/or predictable earnings are more value relevant, i.e. increase the association of earnings and stock prices (e.g., Lipe, 1990; Kormendi/Lipe, 1987; Easton/Zmijewski, 1989).

Current earnings are usually regressed on the lagged earnings to assess earnings predictability and earnings persistence (e.g., Lev, 1983; Ali/Zarowin, 1992).[4] In this specification the autoregressive coefficient on lagged earnings measures the extent to which earnings realisations persist in future earnings. The values of the autoregressive coefficient vary between zero and one. A value of zero indicates fully transitory earnings and a value of one fully persistent earnings. The nearer the coefficient to one, the higher is the quality of earnings. The residuals from the autoregressive model are earnings shocks. The predictability of earnings is then measured as the variance of these shocks (Lipe, 1990). If the variance of residuals is zero then the past earnings realisations perfectly predict current earnings realisations. Increasing values of variance indicate deteriorating earnings quality.

---

[4] Higher order autoregressive models are used by, e.g., Baginski et al. (1999).

2.1.2.2 ACCRUAL QUALITY

Accruals are all accounting entries that modify cash flows for financial reporting purposes to arrive at a summary measure of firm performance for a finite period. A typical example for accruals are receivables. The sale of goods on account is recorded as revenues in the financial statements. To reconcile this accounting treatment with the lack of cash receipts, an accrual – in this case receivables – is used. Depreciation is another example, as depreciation serves to allocate a cash payment for an asset to the respective accounting periods in which this asset is used.

Accruals arise as a result of accounting process. They are an unavoidable part of every accounting system. The role of accruals in financial reporting has been addressed in numerous studies (e.g., Watts, 1977; Bowen et al., 1987; Dechow, 1994). From the positive perspective the accrual accounting process is superior to the more simple cash accounting as earnings (versus operating cash flows by itself) are a better predictor of future cash flows (measured either directly or indirectly). In the case of direct measurement of future cash flows, earnings were shown to be a better predictor of observed cash flows pattern of the next period. Dechow et al. (1998) provide evidence of current period earnings being a better predictor of future cash flows than current period cash flows. In the case of indirect measurement of future cash flows, earnings were shown to have a better association with the (changes in) firm value or in other words with the present value of expected net cash flows. Dechow (1994) shows that earnings explain a larger part of stock returns than cash flows. As the difference between earnings and cash flows are accounting accruals,[5] an increase in explanatory power can be attributed to them.

The discussion shows that accounting research found several justifications for accrual accounting. However, accrual accounting introduces a number of problems. It is complicated as it requires making judgments about the cash in- and outflows over time. These judgements can be wrong either because of errors due to the complexity of the business environment and managerial mistakes (unintentional errors) or due to the incentive to show a desirable profit figure (intentional errors). These errors reduce the quality of accruals and therefore reported earnings. The following three concepts measure accrual quality: (1) magnitude of accounting accruals or their relation to operating cash flows in the form of a ratio (e.g., Penman, 2001, p. 611), (2) the accrual estimation error (Dechow/Dichev, 2002) and (3) discretionary accruals (e.g., Healy, 1985; Jones, 1991).

Books on financial analysis argue that earnings "closer to cash" (i.e. which have a small accrual component) are a desired outcome of the accounting process (e.g., Pen-

[5] Some authors e.g., Jones (1991) and Dechow et al. (1995) use the "term total" accruals to describe the same measure. Both terms will be used interchangeably for the change in working capital less depreciation and amortization expense.

man, 2001). As noted above, accrual accounting attempts to recognise future cash flows in current earnings to arrive at a better measure of firm performance. The process involves accruing expected future cash flows and deferring the cash flows of the past period(s), which requires a lot of judgment. Therefore, accruals are a trade off between relevance and reliability. Relevance is attained through the information content in accruals about future cash flows. However, errors in judgments make accruals less reliable than cash flows. Sloan (1996) shows, for example, that the accrual component of earnings is less persistent than the cash flow component as the errors in accruals tend to reverse. As earnings quality is viewed (although not directly defined) by Sloan (1996) as earnings persistence, the magnitude of accruals is an inverse measure of earnings quality (i.e. earnings quality decreases with the magnitude of accruals). The same notion can be found in Leuz et al. (2003). Their measure is a "firm specific" magnitude of total accruals that is obtained by dividing accounting accruals by operating cash flows. A similar measure, the ratio of cash flow from operations to earnings, can be found in Penman (2001, p. 611). Intentional errors (e.g., understatement of the allowance for bad debt) in financial reporting increase the ratio and indicate of low quality earnings (Leuz et al., 2003).

Discretionary accruals are probably the most commonly used empirical construct to measure earnings quality. The concept sets forth that accruals (e.g., changes in working capital or working capital accruals less depreciation and amortization expense) can be split into two components: discretionary (managed) and nondiscretionary (unmanaged) accruals. Unmanaged accruals are the "normal" part of earnings that results from the neutral application of accounting rules. Managerial incentives, e.g. an inducement to show a desired level of earnings affect judgments in financial reporting. Consequently, managed accruals are those caused by conservative or aggressive accounting policy choices.

Neither discretionary nor nondiscretionary accruals are directly observable and have to be estimated using accounting data. The models that split accruals into their components are manifold. Chapter 3 will present a review of such models. The initial approach was developed by McNichols/Wilson (1988). According to McNichols (2000) the currently favoured estimation technique is the regression of total accruals on accounting fundamentals that are supposed to drive the accrual process (e.g., Jones, 1991, Dechow et al., 1995). Jones (1991) was the first to use this approach. Following Kaplan (1985), she argues that accruals depend on firm specific circumstances that can be proxied by changes in revenues (that drive working capital accruals) and property plant and equipment (that drives total depreciation expense). The unexplained part of the variation in total accruals (i.e. the regression residual) or in other words the forecast error (used in the firm level time-series estimation) is a discretionary accrual component. Therefore, some authors refer to discretionary accruals as abnormal accruals because they are a part of variation in accounting accruals that cannot be explained (e.g., Peasnell et al., 2000; Xie, 2001). The explained part of the variation in total accruals are nondiscretionary accruals. An estimate of discretionary accruals is an inverse measure of earnings quality. Earnings have low quality if their estimated discretionary component is relatively large.

Dechow/Dichev (2002) assess to what extent working capital accruals map into the realisations of operating cash flows. The authors show that the current period working capital accruals can be empirically related to the cash flows from operations of the preceding, the current and the next period. The accrual estimation error is the part of the variation in working capital accruals that cannot be explained by the realisations of cash flows. High accrual and earnings quality is inversely related to the magnitude of the accrual estimation error that can result both from intentional and unintentional mistakes in judgments about cash flow realisations. The analysis is performed by regressing the working capital accruals on lagged, current and next-period operating cash flows. The measure of quality is then either the absolute value of regression residuals (Francis et al., 2002) or the standard deviation of regression residuals (Dechow/Dichev, 2002). Residuals are calculated from cross-sectional or time-series model specifications.

2.1.2.3 Earnings Smoothing[6]

Earnings smoothing has been defined in numerous ways. A general definition can be found in Copeland (1968, p. 101): "Smoothing moderates year-to-year fluctuations in income by shifting earnings from peak years to less successful periods". A smoothed earnings pattern can be achieved through operating and accounting decisions. Business decisions affect cash flows. An example is earnings smoothing through the use of hedging with financial instruments (Pincus/Rajgopal, 2002) or through control of underlying economic events e.g., selection of projects (Kamin/Ronen, 1978) and altering the firms' production (Koch, 1981). Reporting decisions (artificial earnings smoothing) are decisions about firm's accounting choices with the goal to shift the recognition of cash flows over time to achieve a smoothed earnings pattern (Koch, 1981). Authors concerned with the impact of earnings smoothing on earnings quality concentrate on reporting (accounting) decisions because they are less costly and more prevalent to achieve the same smoothing objective (e.g, Koch, 1981; Fields et al., 2001).

Indicators of earnings smoothing are manifold. Moses (1987) uses a measure of deviation of absolute difference between pre-manipulated earnings and expected earnings from the absolute difference between reported earnings and expected earnings. Positive values of this metric indicate smoothing. Albrecht/Richardson (1990) use the ratio of the coefficient of variation in income to the coefficient of variation in sales.

[6] Earnings smoothing can be alternatively defined as a time-series property of earnings, i.e. earnings variability over time (Schipper/Vincent, 2003). Here, earnings smoothing is treated as a result of earnings manipulation (i.e. discretionary actions that aim to hide economic performance) and is regarded as an independent earnings quality concept.

Values of the ratio in excess of one indicate earnings smoothing. A comparable metric (the ratio of standard deviation in operating income to the standard deviation in operating cash flows with low values indicating earnings smoothing) is employed by e.g., Leuz et al. (2003). Insights in e.g., Dechow (1994) and Dechow et al. (1998) into the relation between cash flows and accruals provide an additional instrument to assess earnings smoothing. Dechow (1994) provides evidence of a strong negative correlation between accrual changes and operating cash flow changes that is a normal result of accrual accounting. However, a very strong negative correlation implies smoothing via accrual manipulations (e.g., Leuz et al., 2003).

The relation of earnings smoothing and earnings quality is not obvious. There are currently two strings of research: The first group of researchers views earnings smoothing as the measure of high earnings quality (e.g., Francis et al., 2003; Zarowin, 2002), the second argue that smoothed earnings are an indicator of poor earnings quality (Leuz et al., 2003; Bhattacharya et al., 2003). The first stream of research defines earnings quality from the valuation perspective, the second from the presentation of economic income. Researchers have both theoretically and empirically shown that earnings are smoothed to communicate private information about future earnings realisations (e.g., Sankar/Subramanyam, 2001; Zarowin, 2002). Givoly/Ronen (1981, p. 175) note that "smoothing can be viewed as a form of signalling whereby managers use their discretion over the choice among accounting alternatives within generally accepted accounting principles so as to minimize fluctuations of earnings over time around the trend they believe best reflects their view of investors' expectations of the company's future performance". Communication of private information through reported earnings icreases its information content, i.e. makes earnings a more useful indicator of a firm's performance (e.g., Subramanyam, 1996; Zarowin, 2002).[7]

The second stream of research argues that smoothed earnings "fail to depict the true swings in underlying firm performance" (Bhattacharya et al., 2003, p. 649). Managers may use discretionary accounting adjustments to hide the true performance for the period. In this case, investors may fail to assess correctly the underlying business model and the economic environment of the firm (Schipper/Vincent, 2003).

2.1.2.4 Loss Avoidance

The previous section showed that intentional errors in the estimation of the accrual component of earnings result from managers' intervention in external reporting. An

7 An alternative view is presented in Schipper/Vincent (2003). The authors argue that management interventions into accounting may be transitory. Kothari (2001, p. 133) notes that "the discretionary component of the accruals is likely to be transitory and in fact mean reverting because accruals (eventually) reverse". Investors, on average, attach a lower pricing multiple to transitory earnings (e.g., Kormendi/Lipe, 1987; Easton/Zmijewski, 1989). *Ceteris paribus*, an extra euro of smoothed earnings brings a smaller increase in firm value than an extra euro of unsmoothed earnings.

initial point of studies on earnings manipulation is a hypothesis about motivations to manipulate earnings. Unfortunately, motivations cannot be directly observed. A recent approach is to link motivations to easily observable earnings thresholds. The first distributional tests of earnings manipulations are present in Hayn (1995).[8] She attributes the discontinuity around zero in the earnings distribution to earnings manipulations:

> "Interestingly, there is a point of discontinuity around zero. Specifically, there is a concentration of cases just above zero, while there are fewer than expected cases (assuming the above normal distribution) of small losses (i.e. just below zero). The frequency of observations in both the region just above zero and that just below zero departs significantly from the expected frequency under the normal distribution at the 1% significance level using the binominal test. These results suggest that firms whose earnings are expected to fall just below the zero earnings point engage in earnings manipulations to help them cross the 'red line' for the year." (Hayn, 1995, p. 132)

Motivations to report earnings above the target stem from the concerns of many stakeholders about firm's performance. The perception of firm performance is often reference dependent. Degeorge et al. (1999) refer to it as the "threshold mentality" of stakeholders. That means that companies that are about to report a loss are likely to manipulate earnings to show a profit. The companies that fail to achieve a target face with the capital market penalties. DeAngelo et al. (1996), for example, show that companies that break an increasing earnings pattern experience an average negative return of 14% in the year in which an earnings decline was reported. Later research documented such discontinuities in earnings changes distributions (Burgstahler/Dichev, 1997), forecast errors and earnings per share distributions (Degeorge et al., 1999).

Recent literature documented a general behaviour of managers to achieve certain reporting targets. Such behaviour is usually attributed to earnings manipulation, which distorts the quality of earnings.[9] Adding discretionary items to small losses to arrive at positive income numbers makes small profits less permanent (Schipper/Vincent, 2003). Thus, the earnings levels just above the target tend to be of low quality.

---

8 Prior research documented a tendency to manipulate earnings to achieve a "desired digit" in reported earnings or earnings per share numbers (e.g., Carslaw, 1988; Thomas, 1989). This research concentrates on the perception of accounting numbers as cognitive reference points. In conformity with the psychological literature, firms are expected to show the round numbers because they are perceived in a different way by investors. For example €0,99 earnings per share is perceived to be abnormally lower than €1,00 per share. Consequently, the proportion of reported zeros as a digit immediately right of the decimal point will be unexpectedly high and the number of nines unexpectedly low (e.g., Das/Zhang, 2003).

9 Alternative explanations for discontinuities around zero in the earnings levels distribution can be found in Dechow et al. (2003) and Durtschi/Easton (2004).

2.1.2.5 Book-Tax Conformity

The idea behind the concept of book-tax conformity is that GAAP usually provides more accounting choices than the regulation on income taxes. For instance, IAS/IFRS allow judgments about the magnitude of allowance for bad debt to be recognised. On the other hand, tax rules may give strict instructions about the amount to be expensed (e.g., only the amount of receivables actually written off during a period). The differences between financial and tax accounting are either of permanent or temporary nature. Permanent differences result from items that affect accounting income, but will never affect taxable income. Temporary (or timing) differences result from revenues and expenses that affect book and tax income in different reporting periods (e.g., bad debt expense, warranty expense). Temporary differences are hypothesized to be a result of managerial discretion in external finance (e.g., Phillips et al., 2003).

Not all book-tax differences result from earnings manipulation. However, books on financial analysis show that "...sudden decreases in deferred income tax assets are also a potential sign of deteriorating earnings quality" (Revsine et al., 2002, p. 654). Recent empirical research provides evidence consistent with the hypothesis that the book-tax differences indicate varying levels of earnings manipulation. Mills/Newberry (2001) show that the differences are explained by reporting incentives (proxied by various incentives of private versus public firms). Phillips et al. (2003) document a positive relation between deferred tax expense and earnings manipulation proxied by loss avoidance (i.e. the companies with high deferred tax expense are more likely to report small profits and earnings increases than losses and earnings decreases respectively). Consequently the book-tax differences can be used in the assessment of earnings quality: A closer relation indicates higher quality. An extreme example of deteriorating earnings quality that could be assessed with the book-tax differences is the case of Enron. Lev/Nissim (2002) note that Enron did not pay taxes for several years before filing for Chapter 11 bankruptcy protection while showing high book earnings.

This concept is expected to hold only for countries with (1) low statutory financial-tax alignment and (2) strong market pressure on firms to report more informative earnings (or in terms of corporate governance widely spread ownership structure). High regulatory financial-tax alignment provides incentives to take accrual choices that will reduce reported income numbers and reduce the present value of taxes. Such behaviour will deteriorate informativeness of earnings, as accruals are then used only to signal tax reduction. Market pressure may inhibit downward income manipulation.

2.1.2.6 Timeliness of Loss Recognition and Conservatism (Accounting Based)

A timely recognition of all elements of economic income in financial statements makes them more useful to e.g., investors, creditors (Ball/Shivakumar, forthcoming).

Timely incorporation of economic income in accounting earnings is achieved through the timely recognition of economic gains and losses or in terms of Basu (1997) "good" and "bad" news. While the timely incorporation of both good and bad news is crucial for earnings quality, there is a higher demand for and supply of timely information on the economic losses. The demand for and supply of a timely recognition of economic losses results in accountants requiring a higher degree of verification for the good news than for the bad news (Basu, 1997). This asymmetry in the recognition practices is referred to as accounting conservatism (Basu, 1997).[10]

There is a demand for conservatism because timely loss recognition mitigates agency problems associated with investment decisions (Ball/Shivakumar, forthcoming). Conservatism reduces the likelihood that managers will take the negative net present value projects and overstate earnings (Watts, 2003a). Overstated earnings are not desired because they may lead to paying higher dividends and management bonus at the expense of debt holders and shareholders respectively. In the case of negative net present value projects, conservatism has a signalling role. Conservatism makes it easier for shareholders to trace inefficient investment projects as the bad news (i.e. results of such projects) are captured in earnings on a (more) timely basis (Watts, 2003a). Therefore timely loss recognition enhances earnings quality.

On the other hand, accounting standards often promulgate the asymmetric treatment of economic gains and losses. An example of such conservative supply of accounting information is a lower of cost or net realisable value for the inventory valuation (IAS 2.9). Unrealized economic losses in the case of reduction of the inventory fair value are recognised in income statement as they occur. However, in the case of the good news, i.e. when the market value rises, unrealized gains are not recognized.

There are two main types of accounting measures of timeliness of loss recognition/conservatism: earnings measures (Basu, 1997; Ball/Shivakumar, forthcoming) and accrual measures (e.g., Givoly/Hayn, 2000). The accrual measures can be further classified into the accumulated accruals measure (Givoly/Hayn, 2000) and accrual incorporation of operating cash flows (Ball/Shivakumar, forthcoming).

---

[10] This definition relates to the so-called conditional conservatism (Ball/Shivakumar, forthcoming). It implies that accounting losses reflect economic losses. One of the definitions of unconditional conservatism is as follows: "Conservatism means that the accountant should report the lowest value among the possible alternative values for assets and the highest alternative value for liabilities. Revenues should be recognised later rather than sooner and expenses sooner rather than later" (Watts/Zimmermann, 1986, p. 205-206). Under this definition earnings are conservative when items are consistently expensed early, revenues are consistently delayed and/or income is underreported by creating excessive provisions on a regular basis. Such expensing, deferring and/or creation of provisions are not necessarily related to economic losses. Unconditional conservatism will not be reviewed as it does not imply earnings quality. From the contracting perspective there is no "...demand for a known unconditional bias..." and "...an unconditional bias of unknown magnitude introduces randomness in decisions based on financial information and can only reduce contracting efficiency" (Ball/Shivakumar, forthcoming, p. 8-9).

The intuition behind using earnings and accruals as proxies for conservatism is that gains under conservative accounting tend to be more persistent than losses (Basu, 1997). Recall that accountants use a different degree of verifiability for good and bad news. By the same degree of verifiability bad news are realized as they occur (by the means of a one-time loss) and good news are realized constantly over time when cash flows are realized. This has several consequences. First, taking into account that firms reporting negative earnings are more likely to have incorporated economic losses into their financials, one can expect negative earnings changes under conservative accounting to be transitory (i.e. the one time losses from the recognition of economic losses won't recur in the future). Second, because of the instant recognition of economic losses and a time delay in the recognition of economic gains, accounting accruals will be lower *ceteris paribus.*

Ball/Shivakumar (forthcoming), following Basu (1997), regress earnings changes on the lagged earnings changes, a dummy variable taking a value of 1 if the earnings change is negative and 0 otherwise and the interaction of both. The coefficient on the interaction variable is predicted to be negative indicating an asymmetry in the recognition of economic gains and losses (i.e. indicating that incorporated economic losses are more transitory) consistent with conservatism.

Givoly/Hayn (2000) use a measure of accumulated accruals to test for the presence of conservatism. In the long run, the sum of company's earnings should be equal to the sum of cash flows. The difference between the two sums – accounting accruals – is expected to be zero. Under consistent application of conservative accounting, however, accruals will be systematically understated. Therefore, negative accumulated accruals (the difference between earnings and cash flows) indicate conservatism.

Ball/Shivakumar (forthcoming) use an asymmetric correlation between accruals and operating cash flows to measure accounting conservatism. The authors show that timely gain and loss recognition will decrease the absolute correlation between current accruals and current operating cash flows (i.e. timely gain and loss recognition is a source of positive correlation between accruals and cash flows). Cash flows generated by single assets tend to be persistent: The bad news (e.g., market narrowing without prospects for recovery) appear as a reduction of operating cash flows for the current period and persist into future (i.e. reduce future cash flows). Such bad news, when accrued, will cause a positive correlation between accruals and cash flows and make earnings more conservative. Authors regress accounting accruals on current operating cash flows, a dummy variable that assumes its value according to the sign of operating cash flows (1, if cash flow is negative and 0 otherwise) and the product of both. The positive coefficient on the interaction term will capture an asymmetric loss recognition and is interpreted as a measure of conservatism.

2.1.3 MARKET BASED MEASURES OF EARNINGS QUALITY

2.1.3.1 VALUE RELEVANCE OF EARNINGS

Value relevance of earnings is the association of accounting income and the market value of the company. "...[A]n accounting amount is defined as value relevant if it has a predicted association with the equity market values" (Barth et al., 2001, p. 79). The idea behind this concept is that the market participants base decisions to trade on the information about the future performance of the entity. Trading activities influence the market capitalization. Not all information is used in the decision-making process: Only information that is relevant and reliable will influence the market value. The association between earnings and share prices exists only when earnings are reliable and relevant to the market.[11]

Value relevance is an empirical attempt to operationalise two concepts from both I-ASB and FASB conceptual frameworks: relevance and reliability (Barth et al., 2001). These two qualitative characteristics of financial statements make them more useful to users. High value relevance of earnings is an indicator of relevance and reliability of financial statements and is associated with high quality earnings.

An empirical implementation of the value relevance concept are the so called association studies (e.g., Ball/Brown, 1968; Collins/Kothari, 1989; Easton et al., 1992). An association study "...tests for a positive correlation between an accounting performance measure (e.g., earnings or cash flow from operations) and stock returns, both measured over relatively long, contemporaneous time periods, e.g., one year" (Kothari, 2001, p. 116).[12] Usually this implements a regression specification with the measure of market performance on the left hand side and (at least one) accounting measure (e.g., earnings) on the right hand side. Two regression specifications are used to assess the value relevance of earnings: price- and return-earnings model. In price models, stock prices are usually regressed on the levels of earnings and the levels of the book value of equity. In return models, changes in stock prices are regressed on changes in earnings and changes in the book value of equity. The choice between the two models depends on the research question and on econometric considerations (Landsman/Magliolo, 1988). The return-earnings model is more appropriate if the research question encompasses relevance, reliability and to some extent the timeliness of ac-

[11] Value relevance studies test a joint hypothesis of relevance and reliability of accounting numbers. If a predicted association between market value and accounting data exists, then accounting information is (at least to some extent) reliable and relevant to the market. However if one fails to find any association or finds only a weak association, "...it is difficult to attribute the cause of lack of value relevance to one or the other attribute [i.e. relevance or reliability]" (Barth et al., 2001, p. 81).

[12] An alternative design is an event study (or information content) methodology. The primary purpose of this approach is to assess the reaction of the market to an event such as an earnings announcement. The primary concern of event studies is the timeliness of accounting information (Beaver, 2002). Although event study methodology is considered to be a part of the value relevance research, it will be discussed in the section on timeliness of accounting information.

counting information (Barth et al., 2001). Timeliness is not an issue in levels specification (i.e. price-earnings model). Kothari/Zimmerman (1995) show that the models have different statistical properties and suggest that researchers should use both specifications to achieve statistically robust results.

Two regression parameters reveal the value relevance of earnings numbers: the explanatory power of earnings and the coefficient on the earnings variable. Higher levels of regression's adjusted R^2 and slope coefficient most consistent with the predicted amount indicate greater extent of reliability and relevance of earnings. The coefficient on earnings is referred to as earnings response coefficient. "...[I]f earnings' time-series properties are such that earnings innovations are permanent, then assuming a one-to-one relation between earnings innovations and cash flow innovations..." the theoretically predicted level for earnings response coefficient "...is the present value of the perpetuity at the risk-adjusted rate of return on equity" (Kothari, 2001, p. 123-124), i.e. 1+1/r for one euro of earnings innovation. For example, *r*=12% is used for the U.S. capital market by Dechow et al. (1999) and for the German capital market by Prokop (2003). In these capital markets earnings response coefficients are expected to have a magnitude of 1+1/0,12=13. Earnings response coefficients that are closer to their predicted amount (i.e. 1+1/r) indicate earnings of higher quality.

2.1.3.2 Timeliness of Loss Recognition and Conservatism (Market Based)

This section will provide an overview of the market measures of timeliness of loss recognition/conservatism.[13] Market based measures of earnings conservatism include regression parameters from event study regressions (e.g., Beaver, 1968; Ball/Kothari, 1991) and earnings/stock returns associations (Basu, 1997).

By the same probability of occurrence of economic gains and losses, only the latter are incorporated into accounting earnings under conservatism. As only losses are recorded, the net assets of the firm will be understated. Under the assumption of efficient markets, however, both the good and the bad news will be priced as they become publicly known. Smaller book-to-market ratios will indicate, therefore, earnings conservatism (Beaver/Ryan, 2000).

An other way to assess the extent of undervaluation of net assets is to use a residual income model (Feltham/Ohlson, 1995; Feltham/Ohlson, 1996). For example, Myers (1999) notes that a positive intercept in the regression of stock prices on book value of equity and residual income implies accounting conservatism.

Recently, the reverse value relevance regression has become a very popular technique to test for earnings conservatism (e.g., Ball et al., 2000). Stock returns are treated as

[13] For a general discussion of the relation of earnings quality and conservatism see section 2.1.2.6.

changes in the prospects of the company with positive returns indicating reception of good news and negative returns indicating reception of bad news (Watts, 2003b). Basu (1997) first regresses earnings changes on market value changes, a dummy variable that assumes its value according to the sign of market value changes (1, if stock returns are negative and 0 otherwise) and the product of both. Under conservatism, bad news will be reflected in prices and earnings simultaneously. However, the good news will be incorporated in accounting earnings with some time lag compared to their appearance in the market prices. The coefficient on the interaction variable is then predicted to be negative. Higher values/significance levels of the coefficient indicate timelier loss recognition and earnings of higher quality.

2.1.3.3 EARNINGS TIMELINESS

Authors arguing that accounting timeliness is a desired property of accounting earnings rely on the definition of earnings quality from the perspective of the economic income representation. Timeliness of incorporation of all elements of economic income in financial statements is an indicator of high earnings quality. Measures of earnings timeliness include regression parameters from event study regressions (e.g., Beaver, 1968; Ball/Kothari, 1991) and R^2 from the Basu (1997) earnings/stock returns associations.

Event studies "...investigate whether a particular accounting number adds to the information set available to investors" (Holthausen/Watts, 2001, p. 6). If an earnings announcement conveys new information to the market, then this will be reflected in stock returns or increased trading volumes over the short period of time[14] after an earnings announcement. A market reaction to an announcement indicates that at least some part of the information in earnings is timely (i.e. was not known to the market before). A higher reaction can be interpreted as an increase in timeliness of earnings or increase in earnings quality.

Similar to association studies, in event study methodology assesses timeliness by the regression of risk-adjusted (net-of-market) returns on the unexpected changes in earnings. The adjusted R^2 and the earnings response coefficient are used as measures of earnings timeliness.

Earnings timeliness can be also measured using Basu (1997) regression of earnings changes on market value changes, a dummy variable that assumes its value according to the sign of market value changes (1, if stock returns are negative and 0 otherwise) and the product of both. Higher values of R^2 from the regression analysis imply a

[14] Period varies from several trading days (e.g., Brown/Sivakumar, 2001; Lougee/Marquardt, 2004) to 60-trading-day windows (Bradshaw/Sloan, 2002).

timely recognition of the good and bad news (i.e. earnings timeliness) and indicate earnings of higher quality.

2.2 The Concept of Earnings Management

2.2.1 Definition of Earnings Management

Recent years saw accounting scandals coupled with the largest bankruptcies in the history of the United States. One example is Enron, a new-economy company focusing on the use of derivatives and energy trading with the seventh largest market capitalisation in the United States. Enron was a success story until the autumn 2001. During the conference call in October 2001, management declared an unexpected write-off in the amount of 1 billion U.S.-Dollars. A write-off was followed by the restatement of equity by another 1,2 billion U.S.-Dollars. In the beginning of December 2001 Enron filed for Chapter 11 bankruptcy protection. This was the largest filing in the U.S. history until then.

The failure of Enron was followed by accounting scandals at Global Crossing, Tyco and WorldCom. These scandals and massive write-offs by other American companies raised the question whether the corporate-profits miracle of the 1990s was a mirage (Liesman/Weil, 2001). The reason for most of these scandals was aggressive earnings management. This section will define earnings management and relate it to the concepts of earnings quality discussed in previous sections.

The definitions of earnings management differ depending on the instruments of manipulation, on the purpose of the earnings management behaviour and the timing of earnings management. The traditional definitions of earnings management comprise:

> Schipper (1989, p. 92): "...a purposeful intervention in the external financial reporting process, with the intent of obtaining some private gain (as opposed to, say, merely facilitating the neutral operation of the process)...";
>
> Healy/Wahlen (1999, p. 368): "Earnings management occurs when managers use judgment in financial reporting and in structuring transactions to alter financial reports to either mislead some stakeholders about the underlying economic performance of the company, or to influence the contractual outcomes that depend on reported accounting numbers";
>
> Giroux (2004, p. 2): "...earnings management includes the whole spectrum, from conservative accounting through fraud, a huge range for accounting judgment, given the incentives of management".

Most researchers define earnings management as discretionary accounting choices within GAAP (e.g., Healy/Wahlen, 1999).[15] However there are other techniques to achieve a desired level of income (e.g., Schipper, 1989; Dechow/Skinner, 2000). *Table 1* provides a classification of these techniques.

Table 1: An overview of earnings management methods[16]

Earnings management type	Specific method	Example
Accounting decisions: Within-GAAP earnings management	Exploiting the available flexibility within GAAP	- LIFO vs. FIFO - Accelerated vs. straight line depreciation - Change in useful life of asset - Recording/taking back provisions
Accounting decisions: Out-of-GAAP earnings management	Not applying/violating GAAP	- Early recognition of revenue (for example, before goods are shipped)
Real transactions	Managing earnings by managing real transactions	- Timing of asset disposals, R&D and maintenance expenses, purchases of inventory (in the case of application of LIFO)

Before turning to "within-GAAP" earnings management, it is necessary to reconsider the role of accrual accounting, as certain forms of earnings management are hard to distinguish from appropriate accrual accounting choices (Dechow/Skinner, 2000). The IASB defines accrual accounting as well as its objectives as follows:

> "In order to meet their objectives, financial statements are prepared on the accrual basis of accounting. Under this basis, the effects of transactions and other events are recognised when they occur (and not as cash or its equivalent is received or paid) and they are recorded in the accounting records and reported in the financial statements of the periods to which they relate. Financial statements prepared on the accrual basis inform users not only of past transactions involving the payment and receipt of cash but also of obligations to pay cash in the future and of resources that represent cash to be

15 The concept that mostly close resembles earnings management in the German academic literature is *materielle Bilanzpolitik zur Beeinflussung des Erfolgsausweises* (Wöhe, 1997, p. 59), which can be translated as the material accounting policy to affect earnings. This definition of earnings management excludes fraud accounting. Similar definitions can be found in Küting (1995, p. 8), Born (2001a, p. 14) and Lachnit (2004, p. 68).

16 Implemented from Bauwhede/Willekens (2003, p. 204) with some amendments.

> received in the future. Hence, they provide the type of information about past transactions and other events that is most useful to users in making economic decisions" (IASB Framework, effective date 1 April 2001, Para. 22).

As it is seen from the above definition, the primary task of accrual accounting is to help investors to estimate the company's performance during a certain period of time applying fundamental accounting principles. There is evidence that reported earnings tend to be smoother than the underlying cash flows because of the accruals that represent accountants' attempt to transform the operating cash flow number into earnings (Dechow, 1994). Accruals make earnings a more useful measure for contracting and/or valuation. Accrual accounting is inevitably connected with making judgments about cash in- and outflows. The question is: How far should the companies go in using their freedom of choosing accounting procedures and when does accrual accounting become earnings management? According to Dechow/Skinner (2000), earnings management comprises "conservative" and "aggressive" accounting choices in the presence of managerial intent to manipulate income numbers (see *Table 2*). Managerial intent is crucial here because "...it would, in many cases seem difficult, absent some objective evidence of intent, to distinguish earnings management from the legitimate exercise of accounting discretion" (Dechow/Skinner, 2000, p. 239).

Table 2: Within-GAAP earnings management[17]

	Accounting choices	"Real" cash flow choices
"Conservative" accounting	Overly aggressive recognition of provisions or reserves Overvaluation of acquired in-process R&D in purchase acquisitions Overstatement of restructuring charges and asset write-offs	Delaying sales Accelerating R&D or advertising expenditures
"Neutral" accounting	Earnings that result from the neutral operations of the process	
"Aggressive" accounting	Understatement of provisions for bad debts Drawing down provisions or reserves in an overly aggressive manner	Postponing R&D or advertising expenditures Accelerating sales

[17] Implemented from Dechow/Skinner (2000, p. 239) with some amendments.

"Conservative" or "aggressive" accounting treatments can be achieved via accounting method choice, accounting method application and accounting method timing (Teoh et al., 1998b).

The choice of accounting method may affect the timing of revenues and expenses recognition. These are the choice of assumption about the inventory flow, the choice of a depreciation method for fixed assets, the choice between direct write-off and allowance method in accounting for uncollectible receivables, the choice whether to capitalize or expense the borrowing costs by qualifying assets, etc. In periods of inflation, LIFO (last-in-first-out) costs of goods sold will be higher than costs when inventory is accounted under the FIFO (first-in-first-out) assumption. The straight-line method of depreciation results in lower depreciation expenses than accelerated depreciation in the first periods. The switch from one depreciation method to another can temporary boost reported profits.

After choosing an accounting method, further discretion remains for the way in which the accounting method is applied. The application of a certain accounting method usually requires some estimates. Examples of such estimates include the estimates of service lives and salvage values of depreciable assets, the estimates of uncollectible receivables by allowance accounting for bad debt, the estimates of warranty costs, etc. According to the former chairman of the SEC, the estimates of in-process research and development by acquisition accounting became a widely spread instrument of earnings management (Levitt, 1998). An ever growing portion of acquisition costs is attached to this account to be immediately expensed. Such a onetime charge will remove a drag on future earnings.[18]

Accounting method timing provides sufficient discretion over when and how events are recognized on the balance sheet. Examples of accounting method timing include decisions about the timing of bad debt write-offs and impairment of assets. Another source of discretion related to timing decisions emerges from fair value estimates that are, e.g., necessary for the application of the lower-of-cost-or-market rule for inventory valuation or the impairment-only approach in goodwill accounting.

Managers may also use "real" actions to achieve a desired earnings level (e.g, Schipper, 1989; Bartov, 1993; Wöhe, 1997). "Real" actions comprise operating and investing decisions that affect cash flows for the period. Examples of operating decisions are timing of product shipments to customers, maintenance costs and advertising. The latter should be expensed as incurred and therefore affect current period earnings. Investment decisions include the timing of sale of property, plant and equipment, and the timing of investing or disinvesting in research and development. The sale of property, plant and equipment can inflate gains for the period. Investment or disinvestment in

[18] In the impairment-only approach, goodwill is not systematically expensed (i.e. amortized), but there is a yearly test for a possible impairment. In this case, attaching higher value to in-process research and development does not make much sense.

research and development (at least in part of research expenditure) should be expensed as incurred. The traditional point of view in the academic accounting literature is that the use of "real" earnings management is not prevalent because these decisions (especially investment decisions) are more costly than "cosmetic" earnings management (i.e. accrual earnings management).

Fraud (or out-of-GAAP) accounting represents an extreme form of earnings management (Dechow/Skinner, 2000). Fraud accounting is defined as: "...the intentional, deliberate, misstatement or omission of material facts, or accounting data, which is misleading and, when considered with all the information made available, would cause the reader to change or alter his or her judgment or decision" (ACFE, 1993, p. 12). Fraud actions that represent an extreme form of earnings management are deliberate misstatements or omissions of material facts affecting earnings numbers. Examples of such actions are recording fictive sales, backdating sales invoices, capitalising non-software development costs under this category and overstating inventory by recording fictitious inventory. According to Levitt (1998) "immaterial" fraud accounting has become a wide spread practice of American listed companies. The IASB defines materiality in the following way:

> "Information is material if its omission or misstatement could influence the economic decisions of users taken on the basis of the financial statements. Materiality depends on the size of the item or error judged in the particular circumstances of its omission or misstatement. Thus, materiality provides a threshold or cut-off point rather than being a primary qualitative characteristic which information must have if it is to be useful." (IASB Framework, effective date 1 April 2001, Para. 30)

To manage earnings, companies "...intentionally record errors within a defined percentage ceiling [usually 5% of earnings]" (Levitt, 1998, p. 16). Although such manipulations are clear violations of accounting principles, auditors tend to define such abuses as immaterial.

The second line that is important when defining earnings management is the purpose of such behaviour. Watts/Zimmerman (1986) consider two types of earnings management behaviour according to its purpose: Earnings management may be used either to hide true performance or to communicate managers' private information. The former is referred to as opportunistic earnings management, the latter as signalling. While signalling increases the firm value, opportunistic earnings management may affect the firm value only over short periods of time (the time horizon depends on the degree of market efficiency).

The timing of earnings manipulations should be considered when defining earnings management as the timing of earnings manipulations can be related to the purpose of earnings management behaviour. From a timing perspective, companies may apply either a long-term earnings management (income smoothing) or a short-term (single period) earnings management. A short term earnings management corresponds to various incentives to boost or lower reported earnings in the current period. Here, earnings realisations in subsequent periods are not of primary interest. For instance, before going public, there is a strong incentive to boost reported earnings to deceive future shareholders about the real underlying firm performance (e.g., Teoh et al., 1998b). Earnings realisations in the years following the IPO will be lower. Another incentive to boost earnings is when earnings fall short of some target such as zero earnings level or analysts forecast (e.g., Burgstahler/Dichev, 1997; Degeorge et al., 1999). There are also some incentives to show lower earnings in the current period. It has been shown that companies benefiting from the United States International Trade Commission import relief investigation manage earnings downwards (Jones, 1991). An extreme form of income lowering is a "big bath" accounting. The theory suggests that when managers realise that the current earnings will fall far below the target they attempt to "clean up" their balance sheets by charging all possible items to expenses.

Single period earnings management is usually associated with opportunism. In this case, earnings management can distort allocation of resources and in extreme cases lead to a breakdown of the capital market (Healy/Palepu, 2001). One example is the overpricing of IPOs. Earnings are managed in the period before the IPO to mislead potential shareholders about the real firm performance (e.g., Teoh et al., 1998b). Prices fall after the IPO as discretionary accruals start to reverse deflating the reported earnings numbers.

Long-term earnings management is the second form of earnings management from a timing perspective. Authors refer to such earnings manipulations as income smoothing or intertemporal earnings management (e.g., Schipper, 1989). It is characterised by "...using unrealistic assumptions to estimate liabilities for such items as sales returns, loan losses or warranty costs" to "...stash accruals in cookie jars in the good times and reach into them when needed in the bad times" (Levitt, 1998, p. 16). Realised earnings pattern will then tend to be smooth.

Most of theoretical and empirical research shows that income smoothing is used to communicate private information (e.g., Holthausen, 1990; Sankar/Subramanyam, 2001). Managers, having the best estimate of future performance, smooth earnings to communicate their private information (Demski, 1998). Permanent earnings are crucial to shareholders because when capitalised, they provide a good estimate of the firm's value. The extent to which earnings are permanent is a function of underlying business model and accounting effects. Income of the company will vary depending on the amount of transitory shocks. Some business transactions can be easily identified as transient (e.g., sales of assets), while others require a supreme knowledge of the underlying transactions to figure out their transitory nature. To the extent that shareholders are unable to decompose earnings into permanent and transitory components as precisely as the management (which is expected to be a case), they will regard all transitory cash shocks to earnings as permanent. Capitalising these shocks together with the permanent earnings will deliver a wrong estimate of firm value. The absolute deviation of this wrong estimate from the "true" firm value will be the magnitude of the transitory shock divided by the discount rate. Earnings management can be used in this case to smooth out the transitory cash flow fluctuations. By applying discretionary accrual choices, managers communicate private information to the market about the underlying permanent performance. Empirical evidence shows that earnings smoothing enhances the informativeness of earnings which is consistent with the provided theoretical discussion (e.g., Zarowin, 2002).

There are, however, reasons for earnings smoothing being opportunistic. First, prior research provided evidence consistent with managers smoothing earnings in response to their bonus compensation (Healy, 1985; Moses, 1987) and job security (DeFond/Park, 1997). By smoothing earnings, the management hides the true firm performance in the current period (Schipper/Vincent, 2003). Investors may therefore fail to assess adequately the firm's business environment and strategy. Second, all empirical studies that provide evidence on informativeness of earnings smoothing are performed for the American capital market. Ball et al. (2000) argue that in code law countries, information asymmetries are resolved rather through private communication than by public disclosure. Ball et al. (2000) use Germany and France as two examples of code law countries. Yet, results in e.g., Leuz et al. (2003) provide evidence on excessive income smoothing in continental Europe. Income smoothing seems to be more prevalent for continental European companies than for their counterparts in the Anglo-Saxon countries. If information is communicated in Europe through private channels, for whom do European companies then smooth their earnings?[19] In the light of this discussion it is hard to attribute earnings smoothing solely to signalling.

2.2.2 Relation Between Earnings Management and Earnings Quality

This section will discuss the relationship between earnings management and different earnings quality concepts. The categories of possible relationships will be discussed first. This will be followed by the empirical evidence which will illustrate the choice of the categories.

According to the nature of the relationship it is possible to discriminate between three types of connections between earnings quality and earnings management (see *Figure 2*). The first type is a strong relationship. In this case, earnings quality directly signals earnings management. Here earnings quality metrics can proxy for earnings manage-

[19] The same notion can be found in Leuz et al. (2003, p. 510-511): "In fact, the evidence for the U.S. suggests that, on average, managers use their discretion in a way that increases the informativeness of earnings(…). These findings, however, may be the result of effective outside investor protection and therefore may not extend to countries with weak investor protection".

ment. The relationship can be called semi-strongly when the earnings quality metric partly indicates earnings management. Earnings quality metrics can then be used with some caution to proxy for earnings management. The weakest type of the relationship is present when earnings quality metrics must be coupled with additional evidence to be able to infer earnings management. Earnings quality metrics alone cannot proxy for earnings management.

Figure 2: Relation between earnings quality and earnings management

Relationship	**Earnings Quality Concepts**
Strong relationship	- Earnings smoothing - Loss avoidance - Accrual quality (magnitude of accruals, discretionary accruals)
Semi-strong relationship	- Accrual quality (accrual estimation error)
Loose relationship	- Value relevance - Time-series properties of earnings - Timeliness of loss recognition/conservatism - Earnings timeliness

A strong relationship exists between earnings management and the following earnings quality concepts: earnings smoothing, loss avoidance, accrual quality (magnitude of total accruals and discretionary accruals) and book-tax conformity. Evidence of smoothing, loss avoidance, low accrual quality (as proxied by the magnitude of accruals and discretionary accruals) or low book-tax conformity indicates earnings management.

Earnings smoothing (sometimes referred to as long-term or intertemporal earnings management) is a form of earnings management because one can achieve smoothed earnings pattern via discretionary decisions (i.e. choosing conservative or aggressive accounting treatment to smooth out fluctuations in operating cash flows). Such decisions will add noise to earnings series and hide the true underlying economic income.

Discontinuities around zero (i.e. loss avoidance) are explained by management interventions in financial reporting to achieve a desired earnings level (i.e. positive versus negative earnings, earnings above analyst forecasts versus earnings below analyst forecasts). Dechow et al. (2003) suggest that researchers should be cautious when interpreting discontinuities around zero, as there are other reasons for an unexpectedly low number of small losses such as e.g., management taking real actions to improve company's performance, selection bias due to listing requirements or problems induced by scaling. However, a kink in the earnings distribution can be at least partly attributed to interventions in financial reporting that represent earnings management (e.g., Gore et al., 2002). Loss avoidance therefore implies earnings management.

Discretionary accruals are a part of accruals (or earnings) that were managed to arrive at the desired level of profit. The most common metric of earnings management are discretionary accruals. The relative magnitude of accruals (e.g., the ratio of accounting accruals to operating cash flows) relates to earnings management because discretionary actions "with unjustified accruals will affect this ratio" (Penman, 2001, p. 611). The use of accruals to achieve a certain earnings target or a desired level of profits is a subset of earnings management.

As the two sets of accounts have different purposes it is evident that managers make different judgements different judgments for financial and tax reporting. One should expect companies to take income decreasing positions for tax purposes to minimize the present value of taxes and the "informative" positions (i.e. accounting judgments that will increase the usefulness of earnings) for financial accounting purposes. Hence, the tax income is very unlikely to equal to the book income. However, aggressive choices under financial accounting framework (that are the attributes of earnings management) will lead to a significant excess of book income over tax income because tax accounting usually does not provide much room for judgments. Hence, a strong deviation of book profit from the tax profit indicates earnings management.

It is important to note that the above mentioned earnings quality concepts are strongly correlated. Leuz et al. (2003) and Bhattacharya et al. (2003) provide empirical evidence of a high country-level correlation between earnings discretion (measured as a magnitude of total accruals), earnings smoothing (measured as a correlation between operating cash flows and net income) and loss avoidance (measured as a number of small losses divided by the number of small profits).

Earnings management is semi-strongly related to the accrual estimation error. As noted in section 2.1.2.2, an accrual estimation error may arise due to intentional and unintentional mistakes in accounting judgments. Intentional errors arise from managerial interventions in the accounting process, motivated by an incentive to show a desired earnings number. The intentional part of accrual estimation error represents earnings management activities. Unintentional errors, however, are not related to earnings management as they do not arise from incentives to manage earnings. As the accrual estimation error cannot be separated into intentional and unintentional parts, some difficulties arise when this measure is used in tests for earnings management. Consider a research design in which one tries to compare earnings management under different accounting regimes. Accounting standards provide a different number of alternative treatments. For simplicity of discussion, consider two extreme cases: lax accounting standards with a lot of alternative treatments on one hand and accounting standards that provide no explicit accounting choices on other hand. Staying within GAAP under the "strict" accounting regime will require applying a certain rule rather than choosing between alternatives or forming an opinion about the accrual process. This reduces *ceteris paribus* the opportunities for earnings management and, hence, the intentional error component. Unintentional error may, however, be higher as the applied rule may imprecisely approximate the underlying cash flow behaviour. Under lax accounting standards the intentional error is likely to be high due to earnings management. On the other hand, management can use reporting judgments to make earnings a better representation of economic performance. So, the unintentional error may be small. Using the accrual estimation error in such an empirical design to test for the extent of earnings management would be wrong because intentional and unintentional errors are negatively correlated.

The concept of accrual estimation error is relatively new. Little empirical evidence exists on the relation of this concept to the other earnings quality concepts. Francis et al. (2002) show that the accrual estimation error is positively related to the magnitude of discretionary accruals (the correlation coefficient lays between 0,35 and 0,68, depending on the way how discretionary accruals and accrual estimation error are measured). The accrual estimation error can be used (in appropriate research designs) as a proxy for earnings management (e.g., Francis et al., 2002).

Earnings management is hypothetically related to the value relevance of earnings, time-series properties of earnings, timeliness of loss recognition/conservatism and earnings timeliness. The relation between earnings management and value relevance depends on the nature of earnings management and the extent to which markets are efficient. *Figure 3* shows these two dimensions and the relation between earnings management and value relevance. Information is value relevant if it is priced by the market. Earnings management affects value relevance of earnings if the discretionary component of earnings is priced by the market.[20]

Watts/Zimmerman (1986) argue that earnings management may be used either to hide economic performance (i.e. opportunistic earnings management) or to communicate managers' private information (i.e. signalling). The relation between earnings management and the value relevance of earnings depends on the purpose of earnings management behaviour. Signalling is a process of communication of private information about future cash flows. Opportunistic earnings management affects future cash flows

[20] The extent of discretionary component of earnings pricing depends on the net effect of discretionary accruals on the lifetime earnings (DeFond/Park, 2001). For simplicity of discussion (without the loss of generality), discretionary accruals in the case of opportunistic earnings management are assumed to have no impact on the lifetime earnings and no impact on security prices (i.e. discretionary component of earnings is not priced).

only in rare cases through the tax savings when financial and tax accounting are aligned to a high degree.

Figure 3: Relation between value relevance and earnings management

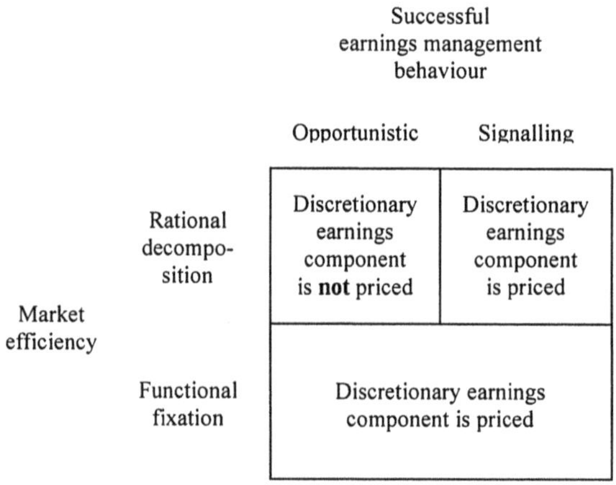

The second dimension is the extent of market efficiency. Pricing of managed earnings depends on the investors' ability to see through the reported earnings numbers. The situation in which markets decompose earnings into its discretionary and nondiscretionary components and can distinguish between opportunistic behaviour and signalling, is labelled rational decomposition. The situation in which markets do not decompose earnings into its discretionary and nondiscretionary components *and/or* do not observe manager's reporting objective (i.e. cannot distinguish between opportunistic behaviour and signalling), will be referred to as functional fixation.

If markets are functionally fixated on the earnings figure, the pricing multiple will be attached to the aggregate earnings figure, i.e. the discretionary component will be priced in the same way as the nondiscretionary component. The form of earnings management behaviour is, in this case, unimportant as the market cannot discriminate between opportunism and signalling. Fischer/Verrecchia (2000) analytically show that a reporting bias (i.e. earnings management) reduces the value relevance of earnings, measured as an earnings response coefficient.

If discretion in reporting is used to communicate private information and if markets are efficient, such behaviour will make earnings more useful. The discretionary earnings component will be priced and the value relevance of earnings will increase. In this case, earnings response coefficients and the R^2 in the regression will *ceteris paribus* be higher. One example for communicating private information about future earnings (at least in common law countries) is earnings smoothing (e.g., Holthausen, 1990; Sankar/Subramanyam, 2001).

The opposite is hypothesized when earnings management is used opportunistically. If markets are able to decompose earnings and know the purpose of earnings management behaviour, then the discretionary component of earnings will be value irrelevant noise that is not correlated with share prices. In this case, discretionary behaviour reduces the reliability of earnings (Barth et al., 2001) and reduces the magnitudes of earnings response coefficients and the explanatory power of earnings (e.g., Harris et al., 1994; Marquardt/Wiedman, 2004).

It is an empirical question to what extent the market can efficiently discriminate discretionary from nondiscretionary components of earnings. Only in efficient markets, earnings management will enhance (in the case of signalling) or decrease (in the case of opportunism) the value relevance of earnings. Empirical research provides, however, mixed evidence on pricing of earnings management and the extent of market efficiency.[21]

Before passing to the results of empirical studies it is important to make a comment on the type of tests employed in the analyses. Most of studies test the pricing effects of earnings management by correlating discretionary accruals and stock returns or by regressing stock returns on discretionary accruals (as well as other components of earnings and some control variables). The pricing of discretionary accruals is a joint test of the extent of market efficiency and the purpose of earnings management behaviour (Subramanyam, 1996). Therefore, finding a positive and significant correlation between stock returns and discretionary accruals is consistent with either markets are fixated on earnings (i.e., markets price opportunistic earnings management as a part of earnings) or that discretionary accruals are used to signal private information and markets price the discretionary component because it improves the predictive ability of earnings. Given the difficulties in disentangling the effects of both hypotheses it is not surprising that sometimes the same results are interpreted differently.

Subramanyam (1996) documents a positive relation between discretionary accruals and stock returns. He builds on the theory that earnings smoothing is associated with the communication of private information. He shows that in his sample discretionary accruals are used on average to smooth earnings (communicate private information) and argues that the observed positive coefficient on discretionary accruals is, therefore,

[21] The following discussion will omit results of the studies from financial industries, i.e. banking and property-casualty insurance (e.g., Liu/Ryan, 1995; Beaver/Engel, 1996; Liu et al., 1997; Petroni et al., 2000). Results of these studies cannot be applied to other industries without loss of generality because "as a result of regulation, investors in banking and insurance firms have access to extensive disclosures that are closely related to the key accruals" (Healy/Wahlen, 1999, p. 375).

the evidence for markets being efficient and pricing information about future profitability. Francis et al. (2003) support the results in Subramanyam (1996) and report a positive correlation between earnings smoothing and the value relevance of earnings.

If markets are able to distinguish opportunism from signalling, then opportunistic earnings management will reduce the value relevance of earnings. DeFond/Park (2001) analyse the effect of earnings management on the pricing of earnings surprises. Consistent with their hypothesis, they find that income-increasing earnings management deflates and income-decreasing earnings management inflates the magnitude of earnings response coefficients.[22] Marquardt/Wiedman (2004) identify a sample of firms in which opportunistic earnings management is likely to occur. Consistent with their predictions, they show that opportunistic behaviour reduces the magnitudes of earnings response coefficients and the explanatory power of value relevance regression. Francis et al. (2002) document a negative impact of discretionary accruals on the value relevance of earnings.

There is a body of research that attributes the correlation between earnings management and share prices to markets failing to estimate the implications of earnings management. Xie (2001) extends the findings of Subramanyam (1996) in showing that the market overprices the discretionary component of earnings. While the evidence in Subramanyam (1996) is consistent with either communication of private information through discretionary accruals or market inefficiency, the evidence in Xie (2001) points to the latter as a driver of mispricing. Chambers (1999) cites the earlier version of Xie (2001) that dates back to 1999 and was only marginally extended in the published version of 2001. He extends results of Xie (2001) by using different abnormal returns methodologies and controlling for risk. He finds significant abnormal returns for the firm portfolio formed using an earnings-management trading strategy. Teoh et al. (1998a, 1998b and 1998c) consider the underperformance of initial public offerings (IPOs) and seasoned equity offerings (SEOs). The results are consistent with the finding that the market overprices the opportunistic component of earnings during the offering year and adjusts the share price in subsequent years, when poor earnings numbers are realised (because of the reversal in accruals).

A possible relation exists between earnings management and the time-series attributes of earnings. Persistence and predictability of earnings are functions of a company's business model and accounting practices. The business model affects the fluctuations of cash flows. Accounting practices influence through the application of (conservative, neutral or liberal) accounting rules. Relationships between time-series attributes of earnings and earnings management depend on the timing properties of the latter. Discretionary accruals (results of conservative or liberal accounting practices) can on the one hand smooth out the fluctuations in cash flows and make earnings pattern, to some extent, persistent and predictable. Hence, intertemporal earnings management or in-

[22] Additional tests show, however, that investors fail to fully understand the implications of discretionary accruals (DeFond/Park, 2001).

come smoothing should be positively related with the time-series properties of earnings. Francis et al. (2003) report a positive correlation between earnings persistence, earnings predictability and income smoothing for a large sample of American listed companies.

On the other hand, discretionary accruals which are used for the one-period earnings management are likely to make earnings more transitory. Discretionary accruals (especially discretionary working capital accruals) tend to reverse over a short period of time. Therefore, management interventions will not stay in the earnings pattern for a long time, what makes earnings less persistent. Predictability depends on the magnitude of discretionary accruals. Dechow et al. (2003) provide some empirical evidence on the relation of one-period earnings management and persistence. They regress future-period earnings on the current period cash flows, nondiscretionary and discretionary accruals and find that the discretionary component has a significantly lower regression coefficient than the other two regressors. This evidence is consistent with discretionary accruals reducing persistence of the aggregate earnings measure.

Proxies for earnings persistence and predictability are used to analyse the power of models that decompose accruals into discretionary and nondiscretionary components (Dechow et al., 2003). Time-series properties of earnings are not used in direct tests of earnings management hypotheses.

The relation between earnings management and accounting conservatism depends on the timing of earnings management. Earnings smoothing is likely to reduce conservatism by delaying the recognition of the bad news. However, in good years, when earnings rise far above the desired level, managers may recognise some amount of bad news (i.e. economic losses) on companies' balance sheets to lower reported earnings. This will make earnings more (conditionally) conservative. Therefore, downward earnings management is expected to enhance the association between earnings and returns in bad news periods (Garcia Lara et al., 2003). It is questionable, however, to which extent earnings-decreasing discretionary accruals reflect economic losses.

Garcia Lara et al. (2003) present empirical evidence on the relation between conservatism and earnings management in different European countries. By comparing two code-law countries (i.e. Germany and France) where one can *ex ante* await a consistent application of income-decreasing accruals with the common-law United Kingdom, where such behaviour is not hypothesized, the authors conclude that earnings management enhances accounting conservatism in the former group of countries.

Earnings timeliness is also only loosely related to earnings management. Timeliness depends on the purpose of earnings management. Only if earnings management is used for signalling, earnings are likely to be reported on a more timely basis. Private information on future cash flow realisations will be recorded in current period earnings and communicated to the market via earnings announcements. This implies that good and bad news will change simultaneously accounting and economic income and make accounting earnings timelier.[23]

2.3 SUMMARY FOR EARNINGS MANAGEMENT AND THE QUALITY OF EARNINGS

The purpose of this chapter was to define earnings management and discuss possible metrics. While there are many verbal definitions of earnings management, researchers usually use certain empirical concepts to measure the extent of income manipulations. These measures are a part of a more general concept of earnings quality. To fully understand earnings management, it is first necessary to clarify which measures constitute earnings quality and how they are related to earnings management.

Earnings quality is a very broad concept that is usually defined depending on the (empirical) measure used to assess the quality. Measures of earnings quality can be classified into categories with respect to the data used to estimate the measure: accounting based measures and market based measures. Time-series properties of earnings, timeliness of loss recognition/conservatism (accounting based), earnings smoothing, loss avoidance, accrual quality and book-tax conformity are examples of the accounting based quality measures. Market based measures include value relevance, timeliness of loss recognition/conservatism (market based) and earnings timeliness.

Despite earnings quality and earnings management sometimes are used interchangeably, only few measures of earnings quality are strongly related to (constitute) earnings management. Earnings management is broadly defined as the use of accounting choices, real cash flow decisions and the fraud accounting to mislead some stakeholders and/or to influence the contractual outcomes. Consistent with this definition, the following quality concepts constitute earnings management: earnings smoothing, loss avoidance, accrual quality (magnitude of accruals and discretionary accruals) and book-tax conformity. All other measures exhibit either the semi-strong or only a loose relationship to earnings management and cannot be used as proxies for earnings management in most cases.

The definition of earnings management is crucial for the analysis. Recall that there are various definitions of earnings management that are different in respect to e.g., the instruments allowed to manage earnings or the timing of earnings management. The choice of an appropriate definition is therefore crucial. First, the researcher needs to postulate an empirical question. Second, he makes a choice of an earnings quality measure (that is strongly related to earnings management) to be used in the empirical tests. The choice of an empirical measure and the research question then jointly define earnings management. The purpose of the section 4.4 is to analyse the impact of accounting standards on the extent of earnings management. Accounting standards pro-

[23] Here again, the ability to interpret the signal depends on the extent of the market efficiency.

vide different amount of accounting choices and are expected to inhibit (in the case of more stringent accounting standards) earnings management. Accrual choice is in the centre of analysis. Earnings smoothing will be used to shed more light on the role of reporting framework. Evidence of income smoothing indicates the presence of earnings management and deteriorated earnings quality.[24] Earnings management will be defined for the sake of the analysis in the section 4.4 as in Healy/Wahlen (1999), i.e. the definition will allow only the discretionary accrual choices. The section 4.5 will analyse the impact of competing incentives on the extent of earnings management. Earnings management will be proxied by a certain level of earnings (i.e. a modification of loss avoidance). For the sake of the section 4.5 the definition of earnings management will include accrual choices, real cash flow decisions and fraud accounting.

The next chapter will give an overview of earnings management detection techniques. The classification of earnings management into accrual management and real cash flow management will be used to present statistical procedures. Fraud accounting – an extreme form of earnings management – is hard to trace. However, some of the models presented in chapter 3 can be adjusted to detect fraud. The discussion of this adjustment will be presented in the chapter 4.

---

24 Recall that for the European countries earnings smoothing is expected to have a pervasive nature.

3 DETECTION OF EARNINGS MANAGEMENT

3.1 DETECTION TECHNIQUES

There is a large number of techniques used by academics to detect earnings manipulations. From a broad perspective, they can be divided into three major categories: simple analytical procedures (Calderon/Green, 1994; Wiedman, 1999), neural network procedures (Green/Choi, 1997) and, the most widely used, statistical procedures (e.g., Jones, 1991; Burgstahler/Dichev, 1997). In the following, it will be shown that statistical procedures are most suitable for research purposes. Therefore, only statistical procedures will be reviewed in the following sections at some length.

Simple analytical procedures are usually described in relation to auditing. For example, Statement of Auditing Standards No. 56 requires auditors to develop some analytical procedures to verify the reliability of financial statements (Wiedman, 1999, p. 158). Analytical procedures are "evaluations of financial information made by a study of plausible relationships among both financial and nonfinancial data" (AICPA, 1992, AU 329.02). These are mostly quantitative analytical procedures that identify irregularities in revenue recognition and aggressive use of reserves by contrasting different financial ratios (Calderon/Green, 1994; Green/Choi, 1997). Previous research has identified six groups of analytical procedures (e.g., Biggs/Wild, 1984; Daroca/Holder, 1985; Tabor/Willis, 1985), from which four are referred as simple analytical procedures (Calderon/Green, 1997).[25] These four measures are: comparisons with the prior year audited balance, ratio analysis involving the unaudited account balance, judgmental trend analysis and judgmental scanning. There are several drawbacks of such procedures. First, they require unique analytical skills and experience from the user. Second, they are not suitable for large sample research projects, where time-series and/or cross-sectional data is evaluated. Third, "they fail to consider the statistical properties of data being analyzed" (Wiedman, 1999, p. 158). However, they can be used in case-by-case in-depth analysis of financial statements, where statistical procedures will not perform well because of the lack of data.

Neural network procedures try to distinguish non-fraudulent statements from fraudulent by construction and training of the artificial neural networks. Different financial ratios are used as input variables for the training. The neural network procedures are rarely used by academics as "...the internal structure [of neural networks] makes it difficult to trace the process by which output is reached" (Green/Choi, 1997, p. 25).

Statistical (or sophisticated analytical) procedures are econometric models used to detect earnings management. They involve the use of regression analysis (e.g., Jones, 1991; Dechow et al., 1995), models based on expected frequencies (e.g.,

[25] The other two groups of procedures (i.e. time-series analysis and statistical regression analysis) belong to sophisticated analytical or statistical procedures.

Burgstahler/Dichev, 1997; Das/Zhang, 2000), etc. The statistical procedures perform moderately well and are well designed for analysis of large data samples. Furthermore they significantly outperform the simple analytical procedures. Wilson/Colbert (1989), for example, show that the number of incorrect signals compared to the number of correct is much higher for the simple analytical procedures. Knechel (1986) and Wilson/Colbert (1989) conclude that statistical predictions and sophisticated models such as regressions outperform the more simple expectation models. However, one of the major disadvantages of such models is their disability of precise estimation of managed earnings, i.e. the discretionary accruals are usually overestimated (Bernard/Skinner, 1996, p. 316).

3.2 INTRODUCTION TO STATISTICAL PROCEDURES

Before describing the models for detection of earnings management practices it is necessary to turn to important features assumed in these models and to classify them. From the broad accounting perspective reported earnings consist of two components: cash flows from operations and accounting adjustments called accruals (e.g., Dechow, 1994):[26]

$$E = AA + NCF, \tag{1}$$

where:

E	=	reported earnings,
AA	=	aggregated accruals, and
NCF	=	net cash flows or change in the cash account.

According to this model, reported earnings may be managed by operating, reporting decisions or by both. If the "correct" application of the accounting policy is in question, then the researcher will focus on the models that detect irregularities in single accrual accounts or in total accruals. For the investigations of discretionary use of the (more costly) operating decisions, academics apply several tests that may detect such behaviour. However, such models are rarely used as cash flow manipulations are studied mostly in connection with accrual management. Studies that lay emphasis on the comparison of the extent of earnings management in different entities or time periods develop/use models which detect manipulations with cash flows and accruals. *Figure 4* presents this classification.

The classification in *Figure 4* is related to earnings quality measures in the following way. Accrual models can be used to detect problems with accrual quality (discretion-

---

[26] Firm sub-scripts will be omitted in this chapter. Year sub-scripts will appear, when they are relevant for the discussion.

ary accruals) and book-tax conformity. Cash flow models detect cash flow management. A combined approach is mostly used to detect earnings smoothing, loss avoidance, accrual quality (magnitude of accruals), cash flow management and fraud accounting.

Figure 4: Earnings management models

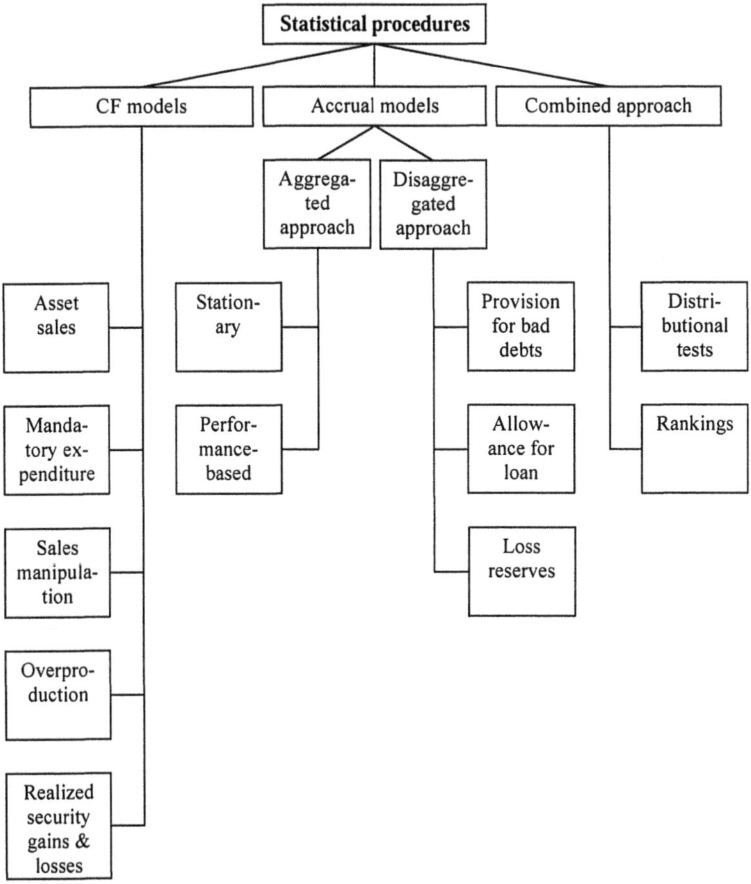

Cash flow models and accrual models directly predict the magnitude of managed accounts. The framework for the direct prediction of discretionary accruals (that can also be used for the prediction of managed cash flows) was first developed by McNichols/Wilson (1988) and will be reviewed in the following section. In the combined approach, earnings management is detected indirectly by using different indicators (i.e. the presence rather than the magnitude of earnings management is detected). Indicators use a sign, the magnitude and/or significance of different statistical parameters to detect earnings manipulations. These indicators are manifold. As a use of a single indicator may cause a severe measurement error, researchers usually use several indicators, which are then aggregated by ranking in a single earnings management measure. The following sections will give an overview of all models from the classification in *Figure 4* and will discuss their suitability (in respect to the power, research design, etc.).

3.3 Accrual Management Models

3.3.1 Concept for the Measurement of Discretionary Accruals

Much of the literature to date that focuses on accruals, uses a balance sheet approach in order to determine the accrual component of earnings. Under this approach total accruals are calculated as follows:

$$AA = \Delta WC - DEP = \Delta CA - \Delta Cash - (\Delta CL - \Delta STD) - DEP, \tag{2}$$

where:

ΔWC	=	change in working capital accruals between current and prior period,
ΔCA	=	change in current assets between current and prior period,
ΔCL	=	change in current liabilities between current and prior period,
$\Delta Cash$	=	change in cash and cash equivalents between current and prior period,
ΔSTD	=	change in debt included in current liabilities between current and prior period, and
DEP	=	current period depreciation and amortization expense.

Accruals can be either income decreasing or increasing. Receivables are called income increasing accruals as the cash receipts are smaller than the reported contribution to income. Depreciation is an income decreasing accrual.

These total accruals (usually scaled by lagged total assets to reduce heteroscedasticity) are then the starting point for the measurement of discretionary accruals. These models split total accruals into a discretionary component, which is a proxy for earnings management, and a nondiscretionary component.

McNichols/Wilson (1988) developed the framework for analyzing the discretionary and nondiscretionary accruals that is currently being used by many authors in accounting research. In this framework, accounting accrual (AA) is first portioned into discretionary (DA) and nondiscretionary components (NDA) as follows:

$$AA = DA + NDA \tag{3}$$

Neither the discretionary component of accrual account nor the nondiscretionary component of accrual account are observable or can be obtained directly from the companies' financial reports. Therefore, authors usually use a substitute, that proxies for discretionary accrual (DAP) and measures accounting accrual with error (η), that is white noise:

$$DAP = DA + \eta, \tag{4}$$

This error is determined by the specification of DAP. DAP is the accrual account less the control for the nondiscretionary component of the accrual account:

$$DAP = AA - NAEST, \tag{5}$$

where NAEST is an estimate of nondiscretionary accrual, thereby specifying η as:

$$\eta = NDA - NAEST. \tag{6}$$

Various authors define accounting accrual in different ways. Jones (1991) and Healy (1985) define it as total accruals, DeAngelo (1986) defines it as the change in total accruals and McNichols/Wilson (1988) as the provision for bad debts. The definition of accrual account(s) under consideration is of critical importance for the analysis. There are two methods in earnings management research for the estimation of accrual manipulations. These are aggregated and disaggregated approaches.

The disaggregated approach focuses on single accounting items that require substantial managerial judgment and that can significantly influence reported earnings. For example Wahlen (1994) discusses loan loss provisions in banks as an important instrument that can be used for earnings management. Beaver et al. (2003) examine loss reserves among property-casualty insurers. A single account has to satisfy three assumptions to be evaluated under the disaggregated framework (Schipper, 1989). First, it must be a good proxy of discretionary accruals. Second, an account must be material, i.e. earnings management via this account should significantly alter the earnings figure. For example, Beaver et al. (2003) analyse the claim loss reserve of property-casualty insurers. This liability accounts for 56 percent of total liabilities in their sample. Third, it must require substantial managerial judgment, i.e. an account must be at least partly discretionary. The disaggregated approach has an advantage of "... yielding precise directional predictions based on the researcher's understanding and analysis of how decision makers trade off the incentives associated with the accounting object of study" (Francis, 2001, p. 314). The disadvantage of this approach is in "... providing a piecemeal, one-choice-at-a-time analysis" (Francis, 2001, p. 314).

An alternative to the disaggregated approach is the aggregated approach. The aggregated approach considers multiple choices or at least the aggregated outcomes of multiple accrual accounting choices used by companies to manage reported earnings. The aggregated approach examines all accrual accounts, because the results of an analysis involving a specific accrual account are not generalisable beyond this account. Jones (1991) uses "...the discretionary portion of total accruals ... to capture earnings management rather than the discretionary portion of a single account ... because total [discretionary] accruals should capture a larger portion of managers' manipulations" (Jones, 1991, p. 206). However, the aggregated approach has several disadvantages. They include, for example, limitations "...of models used to detect accrual manipulation and limitations of the ability of the accruals approach to address the portfolio of accounting choices that managers make" (Francis, 2001, p. 314).

Under the aggregated approach, accrual models can be classified into two groups: stationary discretionary accruals models and performance-based discretionary accruals models. Researchers that use stationary discretionary accruals models assume that nondiscretionary accruals follow a white noise (Healy, 1985) or a random walk process (DeAngelo, 1986) and, therefore, do not depend on the changes in the economic conditions of the firm (e.g., increase in sales or investments). There are four stationary models that were used in the academic accounting research: the Healy model (Healy, 1985), the DeAngelo model (DeAngelo, 1986), the Components model (Thomas/Zhang, 2000) and the Industry model (Dechow/Sloan, 1991).

Kaplan (1985) suggests that nondiscretionary accruals are highly dependent on the firm's financial performance, and therefore should vary with the changes in economic circumstances. Performance-based discretionary accruals models control for these changes. Performance-based models are based on the prediction of nondiscretionary accruals with the help of ordinary least squares (OLS) regression (e.g., Jones, 1991) or more sophisticated generalized method of moments approaches (Kang/Sivaramakrishnan, 1995). Performance-based discretionary accruals models are manifold. Jones (1991) pioneered the development of such models. Since 1991, her original model was modified with respect to the right-hand-side variables (Teoh et al., 1998c; Peasnell et al., 2000), the left-hand-side variables (e.g., Dechow et al., 1995; Shivakumar, 1996; Kothari et al., 2002), estimation data sets (DeFond/Jiambalvo, 1994) and estimation procedure (Kang/Sivaramakrishnan, 1995).

Most of the models that will be described afterwards require the researcher to use a so called "estimation period", in which the author predicts no systematic earnings management (Dechow et al., 1995).[27] The estimation period is used to evaluate the model's parameters, which are then used in the event period to measure the magnitude of earnings management. The separation of the sample period into estimation and event periods is a part of the "traditional" approach to the measurement of earnings management. Under this framework, the time-series of firm observations are centred at some event, e.g. initial public offering (Teoh et al., 1998b) or import relief investigation (Jones, 1991), when earnings management is predicted. Model parameters are evaluated over the time before the event (i.e. during the estimation period). The presence of predicted earnings management is tested using estimated model parameters in the event period. Speaking in terms of regression analysis: (1) the coefficients are estimated in the estimation period, (2) these coefficients are used to predict the level of nondiscretionary accrual component in the test period, and (3) the prediction error (in the test period) is a proxy for the discretionary component. Subsequent sections will present the models in the "event period form".

Some research designs, however, have an overlapping estimation and event periods (e.g., Subramanyam, 1996). Here, model parameters and earnings management are evaluated over the same sample period. Speaking in terms of regression analysis: (1) the model is fitted over the sample period, (2) the fitted values proxy for the nondiscretionary component, and (3) regression residuals proxy for the discretionary component.

3.3.2 Disaggregated Approach

3.3.2.1 Bad Debt Provisions

The accrual accounts that have been intensively studied using the disaggregated approach are the bad debt provisions (McNichols/Wilson, 1988), the provision/allowance for loan losses (Wahlen, 1994; Beaver/Engel, 1996) and loss reserves (Petroni, 1992; Beaver et al., 2003). Most of the studies examined these accounts for certain industries (e.g., banking sector (Wahlen, 1994; Beaver/Engel, 1996) and property-casualty insurance industry (Petroni, 1992; Beaver et al., 2003)) for better model specification.

The first authors to examine earnings management activities using disaggregated approach were McNichols/Wilson (1988). Authors modelled the provision for bad debt in the following way:

$$\text{BgBl} + \text{PROV} - \text{WriteOffs} = \text{EndBl}, \tag{7}$$

[27] In Healy (1985) the "estimation period" is a group, in which earnings management is predicted to be managed upwards.

where:

BgBl	=	beginning balance allowance for bad debts,
PROV	=	provision for bad debts,
WriteOffs	=	write-offs for the period, and
EndBl	=	ending balance provision for bad debts.

McNichols/Wilson argue that there are three variables which can predict the nondiscretionary component of the provision for bad debts. These are allowance's beginning balance, write-offs of the current period and write-offs of the following period (as the proxy for management's expectation of future write-offs):

$$NDPROV_{\tau} = a_1 + a_2 BgBl_{\tau} + a_3 WriteOffs_{\tau} + a_4 WriteOffs_{\tau+1},^{28} \qquad (8)$$

where:

$NDPROV_{\tau}$	=	nondiscretionary provision for bad debts,
a_1, a_2, a_3, a_4	=	estimates of firm specific parameters, and
τ	=	a year subscript indicating a year in the event period.

OLS is used to obtain estimates a_1, a_2, a_3 and a_4 of firm specific parameters α_1, α_2, α_3 and α_4 from the firm sample in the estimation period:

$$PROV_t = \alpha_1 + \alpha_2 BgBl_t + \alpha_3 WriteOffs_t + \alpha_4 WriteOffs_{t+1} + \varepsilon_t, \qquad (9)$$

where:

$\alpha_1, \alpha_2, \alpha_3, \alpha_4$	=	firm specific parameters, and
t	=	a year subscript indicating a year in the estimation period.

The first difference between the event period's nondiscretionary provision determined by (8) and the balance sheet provision is a proxy for earnings management (i.e. the prediction error).

Alternatively, in a research design with no separation of estimation and event periods, the predicted part of (9), i.e. $a_1 + a_2 BgBl_t + a_3 WriteOffs_t + a_4 WriteOffs_{t+1}$ (with t being *here* a year subscript indicating a year in the sample period), proxies for nondiscretionary provision and the regression residual ε_t proxies for the discretionary part of provision.

---

[28] All variables are deflated by the sales in period τ.

3.2.2.2 PROVISION AND ALLOWANCE FOR LOAN LOSSES

Wahlen (1994) proposes a model for the estimation of discretionary provision for loan losses in the banking sector.[29] In the first step, he predicts the change in non-performing bank loans:

$$\Delta NPL_t = \alpha_1 + \sum_{j=1}^{6} \alpha_{2j} LOut_{jt-1} + \alpha_3 \Delta NPL_{t-1} + \varepsilon_t , \qquad (10)$$

where:

$\Delta NPL_{t \text{ or } t-1}$	=	the change in non-performing loans, and
$LOut_{jt-1}$	=	beginning balances of loans in six categories: commercial, consumer, real estate, foreign, loans to other financial institutions, and other loans.

OLS is used to obtain estimates a_1, a_2, a_3 and a_4 of bank specific parameters α_1, α_2, α_3 and α_4 from the firm sample in the estimation period. The expected change in non-performing bank loans is used with the other variables to predict the nondiscretionary provision:

$$NDLLP_\tau = b_1 + \sum_{j=1}^{6} b_{2j} LOut_{j\tau-1} + b_3 E\Delta NPL_\tau + b_4 NPL_{\tau-1} + b_5 LLA_{\tau-1} ,^{30} \qquad (11)$$

where:

$NDLLP_\tau$	=	nondiscretionary loan loss provision,
$E\Delta NPL_\tau$	=	expected change in non-performing loans, estimated using equation (10), and
$LLA_{\tau-1}$	=	the beginning balance in the loan loss allowance account.

Four variables are used in the model to predict the expected level of loan loss provision (i.e. the nondiscretionary loan loss provision). First, the beginning balance of loans, which is decomposed into six categories with the unique default risk. Loans should have appropriate (different) weights for better prediction of nondiscretionary loan loss provision. Two other variables – the lagged non-performing loans and the expected change in non-performing loans of the current period – are included to control for prior and future changes in non-performing loans, which drive potential loan losses and influence the amount of provision. The lagged loan loss allowance is added to proxy for prior provisions.

[29] Provision for loan losses is the amount needed to be credited to the allowance account at the end of the period to make the allowance show 'adequate' values (Beaver/Engel, 1996).

[30] Variables are scaled by the lagged market value of equity.

Additionally, Wahlen (1994) models the nondiscretionary portion of loan charge-offs as:

$$NDLCO_\tau = c_1 + \sum_{j=1}^{6} c_{2j} LoansOut_{j\tau-1} + c_3 E\Delta NPL_\tau + c_4 NPL_{\tau-1} + c_5 LLA_{\tau-1}, \quad (12)$$[31]

where:
$NDLCO_\tau$ = nondiscretionary loan charge-offs.

Beatty et al. (2002) model nondiscretionary loan loss provisions similar to Wahlen (1994) and Beatty et al. (1995). They add the logarithm of total assets to control for size-related effects. The following equation is used to predict the nondiscretionary loan loss provision:

$$NDLLP_\tau = a_1 + \sum_{j=1}^{6} a_{2j} Loans_{j\tau-1} + a_3 \ln(A_\tau) + a_4 \Delta NPL_\tau + a_5 LLA_\tau, \quad (13)$$[32]

where:
$Loans_{jt-1}$ = beginning balances of loans in six categories as a percentage of total loans: commercial and industrial loans, loans secured by real estate, loans to depositary institutions, loans to finance agricultural production, loans to foreign governments, loans to individuals, and
A_τ = total assets.

Beaver/Engel (1996) use a different approach. Instead of decomposing the provision for loan losses, they estimate the discretionary component of allowance for loan losses account. They predict the level of nondiscretionary allowance using four explanatory variables:

$$NDLLA_\tau = a_1 + a_2 CO_\tau + a_3 Loans_\tau + a_4 NPL_\tau + a_4 \Delta NPL_{\tau+1}, \quad (14)$$

where:
$NDLLA_\tau$ = nondiscretionary loan loss allowance, and
CO_τ = net charge-offs.

[31] Variables are scaled by the lagged market value of equity.
[32] The nondiscretionary loan loss provision and the change in non-performing loans are measured as percentage of the average of total loans at the beginning and at the end of the year.

There are some key elements that differentiate this model from the two above-mentioned models. First, the authors do not decompose outstanding loans. Instead of using expected change in non-performing loans, Beaver/Engel (1996) suggest a change in non-performing loans between the event and the next period as a better proxy for management's expectations. Authors also do not use beginning balance of loan loss allowance. They argue that the explanatory variables used in the model are endogenous (Beaver/Engel, 1996). Loan loss allowance is, however, an account that may contain a sufficient discretionary portion. The discretionary portion of this variable could cause extra bias.

3.3.2.3 Loss Reserves

A group of researchers studied the claim loss reserves of property-casualty insurers (e.g., Petroni 1992; Beaver et al., 2003). This accrual account represents on average 56% of total liabilities of insurance companies and provides sufficient place for managerial judgment (Beaver et al., 2003).

Required disclosures for claim loss reserves provide an opportunity to calculate an 'ex post' proxy for discretionary accruals directly from the insurers' financial statements. Insurers match claim losses to the related insurance premium revenues in the period the latter are recognised. These original estimates of loss claims are then revised as the time passes and a precise information about the underlying loss claim cash outflows becomes available. Usually during the five year period all information about the 'true' claim expenses becomes available (Petroni, 1992). Petroni (1992) and Beaver et al. (2003) use the disclosure of the year-by-year revisions to estimate discretionary accruals in the event period:

$$DREVIS_{\tau+5;\tau} = (RES_{\tau+5;\tau} - RES_{\tau;\tau})/A_{\tau}, \qquad (15)$$

where:

$DREVIS_{\tau+5;\tau}$	=	(discretionary) reserve revision,
$RES_{\tau;\tau}$	=	loss reserve for year τ reported in the year τ, and
$RES_{\tau+5;\tau}$	=	the revised estimate of the year τ loss reserve reported in the year $\tau+5$.

A non-zero first difference between year $\tau+5$ revised estimate of year τ reserve and the year τ claim loss reserve indicates the presence of earnings management.

Petroni (1992) and Beaver et al. (2003) use the revision in reserve as a proxy for earnings management (i.e. they suppose that reserve revision results solely from prior discretion in estimating loss liability). However, Petroni et al. (2000) argue that a part of it is nondiscretionary. They decompose the reserve with the help of proxies for discretionary and nondiscretionary behaviour into three components: discretionary revision, nondiscretionary revision and residual revision (see model (16)).

$$\begin{aligned} REVIS_{\tau+h;\tau} &= a_1 + b_1 NOL_\tau + b_2 Cap_\tau + b_3 ROA_\tau \\ &+ c_1 Tail_\tau + c_2 LTail_\tau + c_3 Wkcomp_\tau + c_4 Auto_\tau + \xi_\tau, \end{aligned} \quad (16)$$

where:

NOL_τ	=	a dummy variable taking a value of 1 if the firm has net operating loss carryforwards and 0 otherwise,
Cap_τ	=	a dummy variable taking a value of 1 if the ratio of statutory surplus to net premiums earned is in the lowest quartile of the sample that year and 0 otherwise,
ROA_τ	=	return on assets: earnings deflated by total assets,
$Tail_\tau$	=	one minus the ratio of cash paid this year for prior year's business to loss reserves at the beginning of the year,
$LTail_\tau$	=	the proportion of premiums earned in the high risk, long-tailed coverage lines of business,
$Wkcomp_\tau$	=	the proportion of premiums earned in the low risk, long-tailed coverage lines of business,
$Auto_\tau$	=	the proportion of premiums earned in the low risk, short-tailed coverage lines of business, and
ζ_τ	=	the residual revision.

The first three variables – net operating carryforwards dummy, regulatory capital adequacy dummy and return on assets dummy – proxy for three motivations to manage earnings: tax minimisation, regulatory scrutiny, and income smoothing respectively.[33] To proxy for the influence of firm-specific economic factors (i.e. nondiscretionary revisions), the authors first classify insurer's business portfolio along two dimensions: low versus high risk and long- versus short-tailed coverage. Three variables are then added into the model (16) – LTail, Wkcomp and Auto – to "capture ex post shocks to the conditional expectations of claim payments" (Petroni et al., 2000).[34] The last variable (Tail) proxies for the uncertainty of claim losses. The projection of NOL, Cap and ROA on REVIS is the discretionary revision. The predicted value of REVIS based on Tail, LTail, Wkcomp and Auto is the nondiscretionary revision. The third component – the regression error term – is the residual revision, which captures parts of discretionary and nondiscretionary revisions and omitted factors (e.g., managerial skills in estimating the amount of the liability).[35]

---

[33] See the next chapter for motivations of discretionary behaviour.

[34] The fourth variable the proportion of premiums earned in the high risk short-tailed coverage lines of business is omitted from the model to avoid perfect multicollinearity.

[35] Alternatively, researchers may regress REVIS only on nondiscretionary accruals proxies. The regression residual will capture then the extent of discretionary behaviour.

3.3.3 Aggregated Approach

3.3.3.1 Stationary Discretionary Accruals Models

Four stationary discretionary accruals models will be reviewed in this section: the Healy model, the DeAngelo model, the components model and the industry model.

The DeAngelo model

The DeAngelo model (DeAngelo, 1986) has been rarely used in the prior empirical research on earnings management (Dechow et al., 1995, p. 198). DeAngelo assumes that discretionary accruals follow a random walk process. Therefore, she uses lagged total accruals as a proxy for expected nondiscretionary accruals of the current period:

$$NDA_{\tau} = AA_{\tau-1} \tag{17}$$

The discretionary component of total accruals is computed then as the first difference between the period τ total accruals and the total accruals of the period τ-1. Under the hypothesis of no earnings management, DeAngelo assumes that the first difference will have a value of zero. If earnings management occurs in the current period, then the model shows the difference that is less or higher than zero and is a proxy for discretionary accruals. That means, that this model will only work if both of the assumptions are true: (1) nondiscretionary accruals are equal over time, and (2) discretionary accruals have a mean of zero in the estimation period. If these assumptions are not true then the DeAngelo model will measure nondiscretionary accruals with error. On the other hand, a big practical advantage of this model is the short estimation period.

The Healy model

Healy (1985) detects earnings management by comparing mean total accruals across the sample firms divided into three groups conditional on the earnings management direction (i.e. upward earnings management and downward earnings management). In the first sample group, the author expects that the reported earnings will be managed upwards. Other two groups consist of companies with the negative earnings management forecast. Conclusions are made after the pairwise comparison of the mean total accruals of the first group, where earnings are predicted to be managed upwards, with the mean total accruals in the other two groups separately. The mean total accruals from the group in which earnings are predicted to be managed upwards ("estimation period" in the model) represent the proxy for nondiscretionary accruals. This assumes the following discretionary accruals model:

$$\mathrm{NDA}_{q\tau} = \frac{\sum_{p} \mathrm{AA}_{p\tau}}{P}, \tag{18}$$

where :

p	=	1, 2, ..., P is a firm subscript indicating firms for which earnings are predicted to be managed upwards, and
q	=	1, 2, ..., Q is a firm subscript indicating firms for which earnings are predicted to be managed downwards.

Thomas/Zhang (2000) suggest a slightly different approach. Instead of the cross-sectional estimation of the nondiscretionary accruals, they propose a time series approach. Under this approach, the nondiscretionary component of accruals is predicted using a 5-year time series for each company. The nondiscretionary accruals under the so-called mean-reverting discretionary accruals model can be estimated as follows:

$$\mathrm{NDA}_{i\tau} = \frac{\sum_{t=\tau-5}^{\tau-1} \mathrm{AA}_{it}}{5}, \tag{19}$$

where:

i	=	firm's i subscript.

The Healy model has the same limitations as the DeAngelo model.

The components model

Thomas/Zhang (2000) suggest that the Healy and the DeAngelo models present two extremes of nondiscretionary accrual behaviour: the random walk and the mean-reverting cases. They suggest that a model that incorporates both approaches with assigned predicted weights may perform better. For these purposes, the authors first divide total accruals into two accounts: current and non-current, because the mean reversion process of these two components is likely to be different:

$$\mathrm{AA} = \mathrm{CCA} + \mathrm{NCCA}, \tag{20}$$

where:

CCA	=	current component of total accruals, i.e. ΔWC, and
NCCA	=	non-current component of total accruals, i.e. Dep.

Then they design two models, where weights are predicted cross-sectionally:

$$NDCCA_\tau = aCCA_{\tau-1} + (1-a)\frac{\sum_{t=\tau-5}^{\tau-1} CCA_t}{5}, \tag{21}$$

$$NDNCCA_\tau = bNCCA_{\tau-1} + (1-b)\frac{\sum_{t=\tau-5}^{\tau-1} NCCA_t}{5}, \tag{22}$$

where:

a, b	=	predicted values of current (α) and non-current (β) weights respectively,
$NDCCA_\tau$	=	nondiscretionary current component of total accruals, and
$NDNCCA_\tau$	=	nondiscretionary non-current component of total accruals.

Predictions for the current and non-current accruals are then summed to obtain the proxy for the nondiscretionary accruals in the period τ.

The industry model

The industry model, developed by Dechow/Sloan (1991), does not assume that nondiscretionary accruals are constant over time. The authors assume that a firm's accrual development can be explained by accruals reported by other firms in the same industry (usually defined based on the two-digit Standard Industrial Classification (SIC) code).

The industry model assumes the variation in the determinants of nondiscretionary accruals is pretty much the same in the same industry:

$$NDA_\tau = a_1 + a_2 med(AA_\tau), \tag{23}$$

where:

$med(AA_\tau)$	=	the median value of total accruals scaled by lagged total assets for all non-sample firms in the same industry.

The model assumes that discretionary accruals are not correlated across the firms in the same industry. This assumption is false when many firms try to manage earnings in one direction (that is upwards or downwards) over a significant period of time in the estimation and test periods.[36]

36 A game-theoretic approach to earnings management suggests that firms manage earnings because they expect their rivals (from the same industry) to do so (e.g., Bagnoli/Watts, 2000).

3.3.3.2 PERFORMANCE-BASED DISCRETIONARY ACCRUALS MODELS

The use of the so-called performance-based discretionary accruals models started with Jones (1991). Currently there are many models that use a company's economic circumstances (i.e. performance) as a measure that influences the development of the nondiscretionary accruals. As the purpose of these manifold models is to improve the power of the 'original' Jones model, they will be classified here as 'modifications' of the Jones model. This section will provide an overview of the original Jones (1991) model and its modifications with respect to the right-hand-side variables, the left-hand-side variables, the estimation period and the estimation method.

The original Jones model

The Jones model is more powerful then all of the above mentioned stationary discretionary accruals models in the sense that it relaxes the assumption that the nondiscretionary accruals are constant over time. Jones (1991) uses the following model to control for the economic circumstances of the firm that may lead to changes in nondiscretionary accruals. The variables in the model are scaled by the lagged assets to reduce heteroskedasticity (Jones, 1991, p. 212).

$$AA_t = \alpha_1 \left(\frac{1}{A_{t-1}} \right) + \alpha_2 \Delta REV_t + \alpha_3 PPE_t + \varepsilon_t \text{, or} \tag{24}$$

$$AA_t = \alpha_1 + \alpha_2 \Delta REV_t + \alpha_3 PPE_t + \varepsilon_t \text{,} \tag{25}$$

where:

ΔREV_τ	=	first change in revenues, and
PPE_τ	=	gross property, plant and equipment.

In the equations (24) and (25) gross property, plant and equipment and change in revenues control for changes in economic circumstances of the firm and, therefore, for changes in nondiscretionary accruals. Revenues influence to some extent accounts receivable, accounts payable and inventory that constitute working capital accruals (Jones, 1991). Gross property, plant and equipment controls for changes in depreciation and amortization expense that is a part of total accruals (Jones, 1991). The difference between models (24) and (25) is in the intercept term. The original Jones model (equation (24)) drops the intercept to allow for a non-zero mean regression residual. Kothari et al. (2002), however, argues that an intercept term increases the estimation power. Both model specifications were widely used in the empirical tests on earnings management.

Ordinary least squares is used to obtain estimates a_1, a_2, a_3 of firm specific parameters α_1, α_2, α_3 from the firm sample in the estimation period:

$$NDA_{\tau} = a_1\left(\frac{1}{A_{\tau-1}}\right) + a_2\Delta REV_{\tau} + a_3PPE_{\tau}\text{, or} \tag{26}$$

$$NDA_{\tau} = a_1 + a_2\Delta REV_{\tau} + a_3PPE_{\tau} \tag{27}$$

The sign of a_3 is predicted to be negative, as property, plant and equipment relates to income decreasing part of total accruals (i.e. depreciation and amortisation expense). The sign of a_2, theoretically, can be both positive and negative as revenues can cause increase and decrease of working capital accruals. Empirical research, however, has documented a strong tendency of a_2 to be positive.

In the event period the prediction error (difference between AA_{τ}, calculated using year τ balance sheet items, and NDA_{τ}, estimated with the help of (26) or (27)) is a proxy for discretionary accruals. Alternatively, in a research design with the overlapping estimation and event periods, the regression residual from (24) or (25) proxies for discretionary accruals.

Original Jones model heralded research on the performance-based discretionary accruals models. There are four not mutually exclusive lines of 'modifications' (see *Table 3*).

The first line of models modified the original Jones model with respect to the estimation data (*Panel A* of *Table 3*). The original Jones model used the time-series of 14 to 32 years to predict the level of nondiscretionary accruals. The estimated regression coefficients represented firm-specific parameters. However, recently some authors argue that cross-sectional approach for the estimation of firm-specific parameters is likely to outperform the traditional method (e.g., Subramanyam, 1996, p. 266; DeFond/Subramanyam, 1998, footnote 10). These authors suggest that the cross-sectional Jones model appears to be better specified and does not have a problem of serially-correlated residuals. In such models firm-years are first grouped according to a two-digit SIC code. Regression analysis is performed cross-sectionaly and separately for each of these two-digit SIC code groups.

The second line of research modified the dependent variable (*Panel B* of *Table 3*). There is a series of Jones-type models that decompose total accruals into discretionary and nondiscretionary components. The authors of these models argue that working capital accruals and depreciation and amortisation expense represent discretionary items and can be easily managed (e.g., Jones, 1991). On the right-hand-side of such models there are the drivers of working capital changes and the level of long-term accruals (i.e. depreciation and amortisation expense): Usually these independent variables are changes in revenues and property, plant and equipment (as in the original Jones model for example). Such models are referred here as the total accrual models. Total accrual models are very common in accounting literature. Examples of such models are the original Jones model and other models presented in the *Panel C* of *Table 3*.

Table 3: Jones-type models

Panel A: Data modifications

Model name	Author	Data
Time-series models	e.g., Jones (1991)	Time-series data (firm specific regressions)
Cross-sectional models	e.g., DeFond/Jiambalvo (1994)	Panel data (time-series cross-sectional regression)

Panel B: Left-hand-side variable modifications

Model name	Author	Left-hand-side variable	Right-hand-side variables
Total accrual models	e.g., Jones (1991)	AA_t	e.g., ΔREV_t, PPE_t
Working capital models:			
- Teoh et al. model	Teoh et al. (1998c)	CCA_t	REV_t
- Margin model	Peasnell et al. (2000)	CCA_t	ΔREV_t, CR_t

Panel C: Right-hand-side variable modifications

Model name	Author	Right-hand-side variables
Jones model	Jones (1991)	ΔREV_t, PPE_t
Modified Jones model	Dechow et al. (1995)	$(\Delta Rev_t - \Delta REC_t)$, PPE_t
Cash flow Jones model	Shivakumar (1996)	ΔREV_t, CFO_t, PPE_t
Beneish model	Beneish (1997)	$(\Delta REV_t - \Delta REC_t)$, AA_{t-1}, P_t, PPE_t
Accounting process model	Garza-Gomez et al. (1999)	CCA_{t-1}, CFO_t, CFO_{t-1}, $NCCA_{t-1}$
Performance matched model	Kothari et al. (2002)	$(\Delta REV_t - \Delta REC_t)$, $ROA_{t \text{ or } t-1}$, PPE_t
Forward looking model	Dechow et al. (2003)	$((1+k)\Delta REV_t - \Delta REC_t)$, AA_{t-1}, GR_Sales_t, PPE_t

Panel D: Estimation procedure

Model name	Author	Estimation procedure
OLS models	e.g., Jones (1991)	OLS regression
Kang-Sivaramakrishnan model	Kang/Sivaramakrishnan (1995)	Generalised method of moments procedure

Another group of researchers argue that managers for several reasons are not expected to systematically use depreciation charges for earnings manipulations (e.g., Teoh et al.,

1998c).[37] In such models only the current accrual component is analysed. On the right-hand-side there are only controls for the normal level of changes in working capital. The Teoh et al. model and the margin model are examples of working capital models.[38]

The Teoh et al. model

The Teoh et al. model is very similar to the original Jones model. Instead of total accruals, authors use changes in working capital. On the right-hand-side there are controls for the normal changes in working capital.[39]

$$NDCCA_{\tau} = a_1\left(\frac{1}{A_{\tau-1}} \right) + a_2(\Delta REV_{\tau} - \Delta REC_{\tau}), \qquad (28)$$

ΔREC_{τ} = net receivables in year τ less net receivables in year τ-1 scaled by total assets at τ-1.

The margin model

Peasnell et al. (2000) suggest a different procedure for modelling the nondiscretionary component of current accruals. The authors argue that their model illustrates the normal accrual process and all variables have a clear economic substance. Depreciation is excluded from the model, as managers are not expected to use depreciation charges as an efficient instrument for earnings management. The authors model only working capital accruals, which they calculate in the following way:

$$CCA_{\tau} = (\Delta INV_{\tau} + \Delta REC_{\tau}) - \Delta PAY_{\tau} + UNIDEN_{\tau}, \qquad (29)$$

where:

ΔINV_{τ} = inventory in year τ less inventory in year τ-1 scaled by total assets at τ-1,

ΔPAY_{τ} = payables in year τ less payables in year τ-1 scaled by total assets at τ-1, and

$UNIDEN_{\tau}$ = all no-cash current assets other then inventory and receivables and all current liabilities other than payables in year τ.

[37] The useful life of depreciable assets appears in the footnotes, therefore, the users may easily adjust earnings for the abnormal part of depreciation expense. Annual changes in the estimates of the useful life of assets may also attract auditors' attention.

[38] Total accruals and working capital models can be estimated using cross-sectional or time-series data.

[39] The reason for modification of the second right-hand-side variable (i.e. REV) will be explained later.

The authors further model normal changes in the single accrual accounts:

$$\Delta INV_\tau \equiv PUR_\tau - COGS_\tau, \tag{30}$$

$$\Delta REC_\tau \equiv REV_\tau - CR_\tau - BDE_\tau, \tag{31}$$

$$\Delta PAY_\tau \equiv PUR_\tau - CP_\tau, \tag{32}$$

where:

PUR_τ	=	purchases of materials,
$COGS_\tau$	=	cost of finished goods sold (including asset write-downs),
CR_τ	=	cash received from customers,
BDE_τ	=	bad debt expense, and
CP_τ	=	cash paid to suppliers.

Given (30), (31) and (32), the equation (29) can be re-written as:

$$\begin{aligned} CCA_\tau &= (\Delta INV_\tau + \Delta REC_\tau) - \Delta PAY_\tau + UNIDEN_\tau \\ &= (REV_\tau - COGS_\tau - BDE_\tau) + (CP_\tau - CR_\tau) + UNIDEN_\tau \\ &= smREV_\tau - cmCR_\tau + UNIDEN_\tau, \end{aligned} \tag{33}$$

where:

sm	=	the gross margin on sales,
cm	=	the gross cash contribution.

Using this equation, where working capital accruals are presented as a linear function of two drivers, the authors develop an empirical model that should predict the normal level of working capital accruals:

$$NDCCA_\tau = a_1 + a_2 \Delta REV_\tau + a_3 CR_\tau, \tag{34}$$

In the equation (34) a_2 represents the mean value of the sales margin and a_3 the mean value of cash margin. The sign of a_2 is predicted to be positive and the sign of a_3 negative. The prediction error in the event period is a proxy for earnings management.

Most research in the field of performance based discretionary accruals models is concerned with the right-hand-side of the equation (24). Researchers argued that changes in revenues and property, plant and equipment are not sufficient as controls for the normal total accruals and that adding additional drivers into the original Jones model or replacing existing will improve model specification (see *Panel C* of *Table 3*). Examples for the left-hand-side variables modifications are the modified Jones model (Dechow et al., 1995), the cash flow Jones model (Shivakumar, 1996), the Beneish model (Beneish, 1997), the accounting process model (Garza-Gomez et al., 1999), the performance matched Jones model (Kothari et al., 2002), and the forward looking Jones model (Dechow et al., 2003).

The modified Jones model

Although the Jones model is simple and easy for implementation, there are several shortcomings of this model. One of the limitations of this model is its inability to use revenues as a proxy for earnings management. Jones implies in her study that revenues are nondiscretionary, although managers may attempt to affect them (Jones, 1991, footnote 31).

The modified by Dechow et al. (1995) version of Jones model is expected to overcome the shortcomings of the original Jones model. The modified model detects also earnings management from revenue recognition. The nondiscretionary accruals in the modified Jones model are calculated as follows:

$$NDA_{\tau} = a_1 + a_2(\Delta REV_{\tau} - \Delta REC_{\tau}) + a_3 PPE_{\tau} \qquad (35)$$

The revenues in the modified Jones model are adjusted for the change in sales on credit. Dechow et al. (1995) imply that managers have more discretion over recognition of the part of revenues from sales on credit than over the part of revenues from cash sales. Therefore, authors assume that all changes of sales on credit (versus cash sales) result from earnings management activities of the companies. If that is true, then the modified Jones model should perform better than the original Jones model. If that is not true, then in periods with no earnings management unmanaged accruals will be estimated using $\alpha_2(\Delta REV_{\tau} - \Delta REC_{\tau})$ although they should be estimated as $\alpha_2(\Delta REV_{\tau})$ since no earnings management in revenues and, therefore, in sales on credit is present. In the modified Jones model, discretionary accruals are overstated when sales and receivables increase and understated when receivables decrease.

Adjustment for revenues in the Dechow et al. (1995) model is undertaken only in the event period. When estimation and event period overlap it is common to adjust for changes in receivables each firm-year observation (e.g., Thomas/Zhang, 2000; Kothari et al., 2002).

The cash flow Jones model

Dechow (1994) shows that accruals and cash flow from operations exhibit a strong negative correlation. Dechow et al. (1995) also provide evidence that the original Jones model is not well specified for the firms with extreme cash flows. Using evidence provided by Dechow (1994) and Dechow et al. (1995), Shivakumar (1996) incorporated operating cash flows as another explanatory variable to control for the normal portion of accounting accruals.

$$NDA_\tau = a_1 + a_2 \Delta REV_\tau + a_3 PPE_\tau + a_4 CFO_\tau \ , \qquad (36)$$

where:
CFO = operating cash flows.

Shivakumar (1996) further argues that the relation between operating cash flows and accounting accruals is likely to be non-linear in cross-sectional data. To control for this non-linearity, Shivakumar (1996) allows the coefficient on operating cash flows to vary across firms. He first sorts the sample into quintiles depending on the magnitude of scaled operating cash flows. CFO in the equation (37) is then replaced by a set of quintile indicator variables each multiplied by CFO.

The performance matched model

To control for extreme economic performance Kothari et al. (2002) use a measure different from Shivakumar (1996). The authors add current or lagged return on assets:

$$NDA_\tau = a_1 + a_2 (\Delta REV_\tau - \Delta REC_\tau) + a_3 PPE_\tau + a_4 ROA_{\tau \text{ or } (\tau-1)}, \qquad (37)$$

Kothari et al. (2002, p. 9) explain the choice of the control by "…intuition (by definition, earnings deflated by assets is return on assets which measures performance) and prior research (studies analyzing long-run abnormal stock return performance and abnormal operating performance find that matching on ROA results in better specified and more powerful tests when compared to other matching variables…)".

The Beneish model

Beneish (1997) argues that the modified version of the Jones model may perform better when lagged total accruals and prior stock performance are added as the explanatory variables.

$$NDA_\tau = a_1 + a_2 (\Delta REV_\tau - \Delta REC_\tau) + a_3 PPE_\tau + a_4 TA_{\tau-1} + a_5 P_\tau, \qquad (38)$$

where:
P_τ = contemporaneous stock price performance, scaled by lagged total assets.

By adding lagged total accruals in the model, tdiscretionary accrual modelhe author tries to increase model's ability to capture the pattern of accruals and to detect earnings management over several years. Contemporaneous stock price performance controls for management's incentives to manipulate earnings.

The accounting process model

Garza-Gomez et al. (1999) use the model of accounting process described by Dechow et al. (1998) to develop a discretionary accruals model. The authors first decompose total accruals into two components: a current (working capital) and a non-current portion. Garza-Gomez et al. (1999) argue that there are three variables that may predict the level of working capital accruals in the event period: lagged current accruals, lagged cash flows and current cash flows. For the current portion of total accruals, the authors derive the following expectation model:

$$CCA_{\tau} = a_1 + a_2 CCA_{\tau-1} + a_3 CFO_{\tau} + a_4 CFO_{\tau-1} \quad (39)$$

Analysis of the autocorrelation function of long-term accruals shows that non-current accruals follow an autoregressive process. Using this assumption, the authors model the normal non-current accruals as follows:

$$NCCA_{\tau} = a_1 + a_2 NCCA_{\tau-1} + a_3 NCCA_{\tau-2} + \ldots + a_n NCCA_{\tau-n-1}, \quad (40)$$

Given (39) and (40) non-discretionary accruals equal:[40]

$$NDA_{\tau} = a_1 + a_2 CCA_{\tau-1} + a_3 NCCA_{\tau-1} + a_4 CFO_{\tau} + a_5 CFO_{\tau-1}, \quad (41)$$

This model builds up the accounting process that „...arises naturally from applying GAAP" (Garza-Gomez et al., 1999, p. 12). One of the advantages of this model is in the researcher's ability to extend it and add other variables depending on the expectations (e.g., non-current assets of τ-k may be added; current and lagged cash flows may be substituted by the first difference in this account).

The forward looking model

The most recent right-hand-side adjustment to the original Jones model was introduced by Dechow et al. (2003). They start modelling normal accruals with the equation (35), i.e. with the modified Jones model. Recall that one of the disadvantages of the modified Jones model is the inability to discriminate between discretionary and nondiscretionary credit sales, i.e. the model's assumption is that all credit sales are discretionary.

40 For simplicity authors limit the autoregressive process for total accruals only to lagged non-current assets.

To overcome this shortcoming, Dechow et al. (2003) first predict the normal part of change in receivables:

$$\Delta REC_t = a_1 + k\Delta REV_t + \varepsilon_t, \tag{42}$$

where:

k = slope coefficient that captures expected change in accounts receivable for one unit change in revenues.

Once the slope coefficient in (42) is estimated, it is used to back out the unexpected change in credit sales. The new model now assumes that only the unpredicted growth in credit sales is fully discretionary. The first independent variable in the model (36) – the cash sales – is replaced with the cash sales plus expected or normal credit sales. The new control for the nondiscretionary accruals is, therefore, $(\Delta REV_\tau - \Delta REC_\tau + k\Delta REV_\tau)$ or $((1+k)\Delta REV_\tau - \Delta REC_\tau)$.

As another adjustment Dechow et al. (2003) add two controls for economic circumstances. Following previous research, authors argue that some proportion of accruals is persistent. To model this time-series behaviour of accruals Dechow et al. (2003) add lagged accounting accruals. The authors argue that the expected future sales growth is likely to influence the working capital accrual levels. To control for such normal accrual development, Dechow et al. (2003) add the future revenues growth. The final model is shown in (43).

$$NDA_\tau = a_1 + a_2((1+k)\Delta REV_\tau - \Delta REC_\tau) + a_3 PPE_\tau + a_4 AA_{\tau-1} + a_5 Gr\_REV_\tau, \tag{43}$$

where:

Gr_REV_τ = revenues growth from the current period to the next period scaled by the current period revenues.

The last line of research considered using a different estimation procedure (*Panel D* of *Table 3*). All models addressed in this section till present use OLS to estimate the regression parameters. Recently, Kang/Sivaramakrishnan (1995) proposed to use a generalised method of moments approach to test for earnings management.

The Kang-Sivaramakrishnan model

Kang/Sivaramakrishnan (1995) argue that the Jones-type models suffer from several statistical problems. These problems are related to the violations of the OLS assumptions. Authors identify the following problems:

1. a simultaneity problem, as "...both the regressors and the regressand are jointly determined by the constraints imposed by GAAP and double-entry bookkeeping" (Kang/Sivaramakrishnan, 1995, p. 355);

2. an errors-in-variables problem, as the 'true' economic circumstances that drive nondiscretionary accruals are not observable for a researcher. The proxies for economic circumstances are sometimes affected by earnings management (e.g., revenues in the original Jones model); and

3. omitted variables problem, as liabilities (a part of aggregated accruals) are likely to be driven by expenses than by revenues. Yet the original Jones model includes only revenues as a control for the normal portion of total accruals.

Kang/Sivaramakrishnan (1995) mitigate the simultaneity and errors-in-variable problems by using the instrumental variables and generalized method of moment estimation procedures.[41] Lagged values of regressors and other lagged income components are used as instruments because they are correlated with the regressors and are (presumed to be) not correlated with the regression error. The Kang/Sivaramakrishnan model mitigates the omitted variables problem by including additional variables: cost of goods sold and other operating expenses.

Apart from the estimation procedure, the Kang-Sivaramakrishnan model has several key elements that distinguish it from the other Jones-type models. The Kang-Sivaramakrishnan model estimates discretionary accruals with the help of the level (versus the change) of current assets and liabilities, as "...when earnings management is isolated in one period, both levels and changes of current assets and liabilities contain equal amount of managed accruals" (Kang, 1999, p. 11). The model also excludes tax related expenses and accruals.

Kang/Sivaramakrishnan (1995) propose the following model for the estimation of the accounting accruals balance:

$$AAB_t = \alpha_1 + \alpha_2(\delta_1 REV_t) + \alpha_3(\delta_2 EXP_t) + \alpha_4(\delta_3 PPE_t) + \varepsilon_t, \quad (44)$$

where:

AAB_t = balance of noncash current assets (net of tax receivables) less current liabilities (net of tax payables) and depreciation and amortization expense scaled by total assets in year t-1,

δ_1 = prior year's receivables turnover $\frac{REC_{t-1}}{REV_{t-1}}$,

δ_2 = prior year's net current assets (less receivables and cash) turnover $\frac{OCAL_{t-1}}{EXP_{t-1}}$, where $OCAL_t$ is all other current assets and liabilities scaled by total assets in year t-1.

[41] Generalized method of moment estimation procedure subsumes instrumental variable estimation. Generalized method of moment estimator is more suitable as it requires less stringent assumptions (Kang/Sivaramakrishnan, 1995).

δ_3	=	prior year's depreciation turnover $\frac{DEP_{t-1}}{PPE_{t-1}}$, and
EXP_t	=	all expenses other than depreciation expense scaled by total assets in year t-1.

Regression parameters in (44) are estimated using generalized method of moment procedure.

3.4 Cash-Flow Management Models

3.4.1 Asset Sales

There are only few studies that have examined earnings management arising from decisions influencing operating variables. The following fields of earnings management activities were studied: discretionary asset sales (Bartov, 1993; Herrmann et al., 2003), mandatory expenditure (Bange/DeBondt, 1998; Roychowdhurym, 2004), sales manipulation (Roychowdhurym, 2004), overproduction (Roychowdhurym, 2004) and the realized security gains and losses (Beatty/Harris, 1999).

Bartov (1993) developed a multivariate model to test whether asset sales were discretionary. The author argues that if earnings smoothing or debt-equity hypotheses are motivations for earnings management via asset sales, then in the following equation α_2 should be negative and α_3 positive:[42]

$$ASI_t = \alpha_1 + \alpha_2 \Delta EPS_t + \alpha_3 DETEQ_{t-1} + \varepsilon_t, \quad (45)$$

where:

ASI_t	=	income from asset sales per share,
ΔEPS_t	=	change in annual earnings per share before sales of assets and taxes, scaled by the share price at the beginning of the year, and
$DETEQ_{t-1}$	=	ratio of the book value of long-term debt to the book value of owners' equity.

This model does not predict the level of discretionary asset sales, but rather shows whether the part of asset sales is discretionary (i.e. the timing of asset sales was motivated by a likelihood of a debt covenant violation and/or a desire to smooth earnings). Consistent with Petroni et al. (2000), however, the fitted value of ASI from the model (45) is a proxy for discretionary accruals.

[42] See the next chapter for the motivations of discretionary behaviour.

A direct estimate of discretionary component of income from asset sales is proposed by Herrmann et al. (2003):

$$\mathrm{DASI}_\tau = \mathrm{ASI}_\tau - \mathrm{med}(\mathrm{ASI}_\tau), \tag{46}$$

where:

DASI_τ	=	income from asset sales per share,
$\mathrm{med}(\mathrm{ASI}_\tau)$	=	median income from asset sales in the same year and industry.

The median value of income from asset sales is subtracted "...to help control for correlation across firms in the same industry and year due to economic factors unrelated to earnings management" (Herrmann et al., 2003, p. 93).

3.4.2 MANDATORY EXPENDITURE

Bange/De Bondt (1998) study only one type of mandatory expenditure – research and development expenses. The authors proxy with the research and development budget adjustment for the discretionary component of research and development expenditure. Budget adjustment is determined as the deviation of the research and development expenditure of the current period from the predicted level of research and development expenditure:

$$\mathrm{DRD}_\tau = \mathrm{RD}_\tau - \mathrm{RD}_{\tau-1}(1+g), \tag{47}$$

where:

DRD_τ	=	discretionary research and development expenditure,
RD_τ	=	research and development expenditure, and
g	=	growth rate of research and development expenditure.

There are several ways to predict the normal level of research and development expenditure (i.e. estimate the growth rate). The authors choose to adjust lagged research and development expenditure by firm-specific exponential growth rate based on a 14-year estimation period.

An aggregated approach to the estimation of the discretionary component of a range of mandatory expenditures (i.e. research and development expenses, advertising expenses, selling, general and administrative expenses[43]) was proposed by Roychowd-

[43] Selling, general and administrative expenses are mostly nondiscretionary. This expense category is added into analysis primary because the level of disclosure often does not permit the direct estimation of research and development and advertising components (Roychowdhurym, 2004). If the latter two types of expenses are not disclosed separately (i.e. when they are not material), they are expected to appear under selling, general and administrative expenses category.

hurym (2004). His model is also more sophisticated as it allows the nondiscretionary mandatory expenditure to vary with the firm's economic circumstances:

$$NDExp_{\tau} = a_1(1/A_{\tau-1}) + a_2 \, Rev_{\tau}, \qquad (48)$$

where:

$NDExp_{\tau}$ = nondiscretionary mandatory expenditure: a sum of nondiscretionary research and development, advertising and selling, general and administrative expenses.

The part of mandatory expenditure that cannot be predicted by economic circumstances proxies for earnings management.

3.4.3 Sales Manipulation

Sales manipulations are defined as managers' attempts to boost current period earnings by providing price discounts and more lenient credits (Roychowdhury, 2004). If sales manipulations are present, then the net cash inflow per sale will be lower. To estimate the normal cash inflow per sale, Roychowdhury (2004) regresses operating cash flows on revenues and first changes in revenues.

$$NDCFO_{\tau} = a_1(1/A_{\tau-1}) + a_2 \, Rev_{\tau} + a_3 \Delta Rev_{\tau}, \qquad (49)$$

where:

$NDCFO_{\tau}$ = nondiscretionary operating cash flows.

The difference between the operating cash flows and the projection of inverse lagged total assets, revenues and revenue changes on operating cash flows proxies for sales manipulations.

3.4.4 Overproduction

Managers of manufacturing firms can also manipulate earnings by overproducing company's products. The fixed overhead, which should be allocated between the produced goods, will be spread between more units in the case of overproduction. This will reduce the costs of goods sold in the period as long as there is no larger increase in the marginal costs per unit. Production costs are the sum of costs of goods sold and the change in inventory (Roychowdhury, 2004), i.e.:

$$Prod = COGS + \Delta Inv \qquad (50)$$

where:

Prod = production costs.

To assess the normal level of production costs, Roychowdhury (2004) first models the normal levels of production costs' components, i.e. costs of goods sold and changes in inventory. Similar to nondiscretionary mandatory expenditure, the normal costs of goods sold are modeled as a function of inverse lagged total assets and revenues:

$$NDCOGS_{\tau} = \alpha_1 (1/A_{\tau-1}) + \alpha_2 Rev_{\tau} \tag{51}$$

where:
$NDCOGS_{\tau}$ = nondiscretionary costs of goods sold.

Following Dechow et al. (1998), Roychowdhury (2004) models changes in inventory as a function of inverse lagged total assets, changes in revenues and lagged changes in revenues:

$$ND\Delta Inv_{\tau} = \alpha_1 (1/A_{\tau-1}) + \alpha_2 \Delta Rev_{\tau} + \alpha_3 \Delta Rev_{\tau-1}, \tag{52}$$

where:
$ND\Delta Inv_{\tau}$ = nondiscretionary changes in inventory.

The normal level of production costs given equations (50), (51) and (52) can be estimated in the following way:

$$NDProd_{\tau} = a_1 (1/A_{\tau-1}) + a_2 Rev_{\tau} + a_3 \Delta Rev_{\tau} + a_4 \Delta Rev_{\tau-1} \tag{53}$$

where:
$NDProd_{\tau}$ = nondiscretionary production costs.

The difference between the actual value of the production costs and the predicted value based on the inverse lagged total assets, revenues, revenue changes and lagged revenue changes indicates the magnitude of overproduction.

3.4.5 Realized Security Gains and Losses

Managers of banks may realise security gains and losses by investment sales. Security gains and losses are the difference between securities' book and market value. By selling certain securities (at the end of the year) a manager can inflate current period earnings. Beatty et al. (2002) use a model similar to Beatty/Harris (1999) to predict the nondiscretionary portion of the realized security gains and losses in the banking industry:

$$NDRSGL_{\tau} = a_1 + a_2 \ln(A_{\tau}) + a_3 UNGL_{\tau-1}, \tag{54}$$

where:

$NDRSGL_{\tau}$	=	nondiscretionary realized security gains and losses scaled by lagged total assets, and
$UNGL_{\tau-1}$	=	unrealized security gains and losses scaled by total assets at $\tau-1$.

Natural logarithm of total assets controls for bank size. Lagged unrealized security gains and losses are positively correlated with current realised security gains and losses.

3.5 Combined Approaches: Models Based on Expected Frequencies and Indexes

3.5.1 Models Based on Expected Frequencies

There are two kinds of procedures that are used to estimate earnings management activities with accruals and cash flows. The first, uses single tests of expected frequencies of earnings (e.g., Burgstahler/Dichev, 1997; Carslaw, 1988), the second uses multiple tests (inter alia expected frequencies), which are then incorporated in a ranking to determine the relative extent of income manipulations (Leuz et al, 2003).

Two sets of statistical tests can be defined as models based on expected frequencies. First, a test for the presence of earnings management using a distribution of scaled performance measures (i.e. earnings and changes in earnings). Hayn (1995) pioneered this field of research. Her idea was then employed for the empirical tests of earnings management by Burgstahler/Dichev (1997). The second line of research tests for "cosmetic" earnings management by inquiring into the significance of the difference in frequency of reporting certain digits as the first-from-the-left and the second-from-the-left digits in earnings numbers. The first to use this line of modelling was Carslaw (1988).

There are several distinct features of the models based on expected frequencies: First, they trace earnings management with both accruals and cash flows as they test for irregularities in the reporting of aggregate earnings numbers. Second, researchers that use these models need to post a hypothesis about a discontinuity (irregularity) in certain region(s) of the empirical distribution in the presence of income manipulations. Third, the statistical significance of this discontinuity is assessed by comparing the distributional frequencies of managed (empirical) and unmanaged (theoretical or expected) numbers.

One of the ways to make earnings management visible is to consider the threshold beating behaviour. Such behaviour will lead to the deviation of observed frequencies of reported numbers from their expected frequencies. One line of the research considered reporting of rounded earnings and earnings per share. In such studies firms are expected to report earnings (earnings per share) that contain "too many" zeros (fives) and "too few" nines (fours) as the first-from-the-left and/or the second-from-the-left most digit (as the immediate right of the decimal digit).[44] To trace the irregularities, the researcher needs to compare the managed (empirical) frequencies of appearance of these digits with unmanaged (theoretical) frequencies of the same digits. As theoretical frequencies cannot be observed, researchers use an approximation for digit's frequencies also known as the Benford's Law (Benford, 1938). According to Benford, the probability of a number being the first (second) digit of a certain number is not equally likely, i.e. it is not a 1/9 (1/10). Ones (zeros) are observed more often then nines as the first (second) digit, which leads to a skewed distribution. According to Benford's Law the probability of the number x being the first digit can be approximated as:

$$\text{prob}(x = \text{first digit}) = \text{Log}_{10}(x+1) - \text{Log}_{10}(x), \tag{55}$$

and the probability of *y* being the second-from-the-left digit is calculated as:

$$\text{prob}(y = \text{second digit}) = \sum_{x=1}^{9}\left(\text{Log}_{10}\left(x + \frac{y+1}{10}\right) - \text{Log}_{10}\left(x + \frac{y}{10}\right)\right). \tag{56}$$

For example, the probability of 5 being the first-from-the-left most digit is 7,92% and the probability of 1 being the second-from-the-left most digit is 11,39%. If the earnings are in any way influenced by the human actions (i.e. earnings management) then the empirical frequencies of a digit's appearance will deviate from the expected frequencies. The statistical significance of the difference can be estimated using the binominal Z-test for a certain digit or a goodness of fit test (i.e. the χ^2-test or the Kolmogorov-Smirnov test) for the distribution of all digits.

Another type of distributional tests was first implemented to detect earnings management by Burgstahler/Dichev (1997). This line of research considers reporting earnings numbers above some threshold, such as zero earnings level or analyst forecast. Here, firms are expected to report "too rarely" earnings that fall short of a threshold and "too often" earnings that are above a threshold. Empirically, such a discontinuity around a threshold can be visualized by the means of a histogram of scaled earnings. The choice of the scaling factor is arbitrary. Usually the lagged market value of equity is used to produce firm-specific income levels.[45] Under a null hypothesis of no earnings management, a histogram will tend to be smooth around a threshold point (i.e. will not show any discontinuity). In other words, the number of observations of scaled earnings in an "unfavourable" interval will not show any statistically significant deviation from the mean number of observations in the two immediately adjacent intervals (i.e. the

44 For reasons of such behaviour see section 2.1.2.4.

45 It is hard to determine what a small profit level is. An income of €100.000 can be extremely large for one company and very small for another. Scaling of earnings figures by a firm-specific size measure (e.g., market value of equity, revenues or total assets) provides a possibility to analyse firms in cross-section.

expected number of observations). If that is not true and the deviation is statistically significant, the number of observations in the bin to the left of a threshold is underrepresented, which is consistent with earnings management. Issues related to the empirical implementation of such kind of tests will be reviewed in the section 4.5.3.

3.5.2 Rankings

Ranking tests usually combine several earnings management metrics in a single test statistic to assess the relative extent of earnings manipulations. This involves using simple ratios, whose characteristics and/or relative magnitudes are easy to predict. Ratios are then incorporated in a ranking. There are several reasons why such tests may outperform other earnings management metrics presented in previous sections. First, a single earnings management metric is likely to show biased results. Recall, for instance, that the accrual models tend to overstate the magnitude of discretionary accruals. Using several earnings management metrics that test for the presence of income manipulation from several perspectives is likely to reduce such bias. Second, ranking tests do not involve the use of complicated accrual expectation models. Third, ranking tests trace the irregularities in reporting of income numbers. They do not discriminate between the real decisions and accrual management, but rather test for the presence of both.

Currently, the most widely used rating procedure is a four-ratio ranking implemented by Leuz et al. (2003). This procedure was used with some adjustments by e.g., Kinnunen/Koskela (2003) and Bhattacharya et al. (2003).

Leuz et al. (2003) use four different statistical measures to rank countries according to the extent of earnings management, two of which proxy for discretion in reported earnings (i.e. a single period earnings management) and two for earnings smoothing. The authors first derive the value of each ratio for each country and then incorporate them in one ranking to characterize the level of earnings management. The four measures are:

1. standard deviation of operating earnings divided by the standard deviation of operating cash flow,
2. correlation between changes in accounting accruals and changes in operating cash flows,
3. relative magnitude of accounting accruals, measured as the ratio of absolute accounting accruals to absolute operating cash flows,
4. small loss avoidance, measured as the number of small profits divided by the number of small losses.

The first measure used by authors is the variability of operating income compared to the variability of operating cash flows σ(OpInc)/σ(CFO). With the help of this test Leuz et al. (2003) try to detect earnings smoothing activities via working capital accruals. If earnings are smoothed, then the standard deviation of operating income will tend to be smaller than the standard deviation of operating cash flows. Smaller values of this ratio indicate earnings management.

The second measure – cross-sectional correlation between changes in accounting accruals and changes in operating cash flows ρ(ΔAA;ΔCFO) – also proxies for the presence of income smoothing. The values of this measure closer to minus one indicate earnings management.[46]

The third measure is a magnitude of accounting accruals compared to the magnitude of operating cash flows |AA|/|CFO|. This test detects extensive use of the working capital accruals to achieve some earnings levels. If earnings are managed via accruals, then the accrual component of earnings will be higher. The scaling by operating cash flows "...controls for differences in firm size and performance" (Leuz et al., 2003, p. 510). In the presence of earnings management the ratio of total accruals to cash flow from operations will tend to be higher.

The forth measure detects management's discretionary use of different earnings management instruments to avoid reporting of negative earnings. Following Burgstahler/Dichev (1997), authors argue that since the number of such instruments and their application is limited, firm's primary incentive would be to avoid reporting small losses rather than try to avoid reporting any loss occurred. Leuz et al. (2003) define small losses and small profits as reported earnings scaled by lagged total assets that fall into the range [-0,01;0) and [0;0,01] respectively. The ratio of the number of small profits to the number of small losses (*#SmallLosses/#SmallProfits*) is used to detect earnings management. Earnings management is said to occur if the number of small profits is much higher than the number of small losses.

Therefore, there are four measures that constitute ranking: σ(OpInc)/σ(CFO), ρ(ΔAA;ΔCFO), |AA|/|CFO|, #SmallLosses/#SmallProfits. To fit into an overall country rating, industries or groups of companies should be ranked by each of the four measures. The summed countries, industries or groups of companies rank divided by four then represents the level of earnings management.

3.6 Summary: Most Suitable Detection Techniques

This chapter provided an overview of earnings management detection techniques. The emphasis was placed on statistical procedures because they are suitable for analysis of

[46] See section 2.1.2.3 for the other earnings smoothing indicators.

large data samples, perform relatively well, and the estimation procedure is clear and can be observed (i.e. there is no 'black box estimation').

The statistical technique that should be employed in an empirical analysis depends on the question under examination. If a researcher is concerned whether certain accounting standards influence the level of earnings management or whether auditors constrain discretionary accounting choices, then the accrual prediction models are the most suitable research instrument. Two types of models were used in the academic literature: models that predict the normal level of accounting accruals and models that predict the normal portion of disaggregated (i.e. single) accrual accounts. Generally, disaggregated accrual prediction models are believed to produce better discretionary accrual estimates. However, the main problem of such models is the analysis of one account at a time. The behaviour of other discretionary accrual accounts is not modelled. Therefore, more general research questions, as those postulated in the beginning of this paragraph, cannot be answered.

Numerous studies have compared the performance of aggregated discretionary accruals models (e.g., Dechow et al., 1995; Guay et al., 1996; Garza-Gomez et al., 1999; Jeter/Shivakumar, 1999; Thomas/Zhang, 2000; Bartov et al., 2001; Iniguez/Poveda, 2004). The evidence from these studies is generally consistent with: (1) performance-based discretionary accruals models produce less biased estimates of discretionary accruals than stationary discretionary accruals models; (2) cross-sectional performance-based models are more powerful than their time-series counterparts; (3) even the estimates produced by the cross-sectional performance-based discretionary accruals models are very biased: Models tend to overstate the discretionary accrual component and to produce inconsistent results in the sub-samples of firms with extreme financial performance; and (4) the Kang-Sivaramakrishnan model does not outperform the OLS estimation procedures.

Theoretically, the best way to model discretionary accruals is, first, to disaggregate the accounting accruals into single components. Second, to predict the normal portions of these disaggregated accounts and in the last step to sum them up to obtain an estimate of nondiscretionary total accruals. However, such models do not exist at the moment. In the absence of such models, the most suitable research instruments are still the Jones-type models. A problem of the original Jones model is the overestimation of discretionary accruals in the firm-years with extreme financial performance. To mitigate this shortcoming authors proposed to control for extreme performance using e.g., cash flows and return on assets. The choice between the Jones-type models (with the performance control) is arbitrary. It is expected that the forward looking model will produce the best estimates of discretionary accruals. However, this model requires a sufficient estimation period even in the cross-section. The dependent variables of this model are lagged total accruals and revenues growth. In the sample period of four years, only one year will be used for estimation (lagged total accruals require t-2 and t-1 accounting data and revenues growth requires t+1 accounting data). The cash flow

large data samples, perform relatively well, and the estimation procedure is clear and can be observed (i.e. there is no 'black box estimation').

The statistical technique that should be employed in an empirical analysis depends on the question under examination. If a researcher is concerned whether certain accounting standards influence the level of earnings management or whether auditors constrain discretionary accounting choices, then the accrual prediction models are the most suitable research instrument. Two types of models were used in the academic literature: models that predict the normal level of accounting accruals and models that predict the normal portion of disaggregated (i.e. single) accrual accounts. Generally, disaggregated accrual prediction models are believed to produce better discretionary accrual estimates. However, the main problem of such models is the analysis of one account at a time. The behaviour of other discretionary accrual accounts is not modelled. Therefore, more general research questions, as those postulated in the beginning of this paragraph, cannot be answered.

Numerous studies have compared the performance of aggregated discretionary accruals models (e.g., Dechow et al., 1995; Guay et al., 1996; Garza-Gomez et al., 1999; Jeter/Shivakumar, 1999; Thomas/Zhang, 2000; Bartov et al., 2001; Iniguez/Poveda, 2004). The evidence from these studies is generally consistent with: (1) performance-based discretionary accruals models produce less biased estimates of discretionary accruals than stationary discretionary accruals models; (2) cross-sectional performance-based models are more powerful than their time-series counterparts; (3) even the estimates produced by the cross-sectional performance-based discretionary accruals models are very biased: Models tend to overstate the discretionary accrual component and to produce inconsistent results in the sub-samples of firms with extreme financial performance; and (4) the Kang-Sivaramakrishnan model does not outperform the OLS estimation procedures.

Theoretically, the best way to model discretionary accruals is, first, to disaggregate the accounting accruals into single components. Second, to predict the normal portions of these disaggregated accounts and in the last step to sum them up to obtain an estimate of nondiscretionary total accruals. However, such models do not exist at the moment. In the absence of such models, the most suitable research instruments are still the Jones-type models. A problem of the original Jones model is the overestimation of discretionary accruals in the firm-years with extreme financial performance. To mitigate this shortcoming authors proposed to control for extreme performance using e.g., cash flows and return on assets. The choice between the Jones-type models (with the performance control) is arbitrary. It is expected that the forward looking model will produce the best estimates of discretionary accruals. However, this model requires a sufficient estimation period even in the cross-section. The dependent variables of this model are lagged total accruals and revenues growth. In the sample period of four years, only one year will be used for estimation (lagged total accruals require t-2 and t-1 accounting data and revenues growth requires t+1 accounting data). The cash flow

The first measure used by authors is the variability of operating income compared to the variability of operating cash flows $\sigma(\text{OpInc})/\sigma(\text{CFO})$. With the help of this test Leuz et al. (2003) try to detect earnings smoothing activities via working capital accruals. If earnings are smoothed, then the standard deviation of operating income will tend to be smaller than the standard deviation of operating cash flows. Smaller values of this ratio indicate earnings management.

The second measure – cross-sectional correlation between changes in accounting accruals and changes in operating cash flows $\rho(\Delta\text{AA};\Delta\text{CFO})$ – also proxies for the presence of income smoothing. The values of this measure closer to minus one indicate earnings management.[46]

The third measure is a magnitude of accounting accruals compared to the magnitude of operating cash flows $|\text{AA}|/|\text{CFO}|$. This test detects extensive use of the working capital accruals to achieve some earnings levels. If earnings are managed via accruals, then the accrual component of earnings will be higher. The scaling by operating cash flows "...controls for differences in firm size and performance" (Leuz et al., 2003, p. 510). In the presence of earnings management the ratio of total accruals to cash flow from operations will tend to be higher.

The forth measure detects management's discretionary use of different earnings management instruments to avoid reporting of negative earnings. Following Burgstahler/Dichev (1997), authors argue that since the number of such instruments and their application is limited, firm's primary incentive would be to avoid reporting small losses rather than try to avoid reporting any loss occurred. Leuz et al. (2003) define small losses and small profits as reported earnings scaled by lagged total assets that fall into the range [-0,01;0) and [0;0,01] respectively. The ratio of the number of small profits to the number of small losses (*#SmallLosses/#SmallProfits*) is used to detect earnings management. Earnings management is said to occur if the number of small profits is much higher than the number of small losses.

Therefore, there are four measures that constitute ranking: $\sigma(\text{OpInc})/\sigma(\text{CFO})$, $\rho(\Delta\text{AA};\Delta\text{CFO})$, $|\text{AA}|/|\text{CFO}|$, #SmallLosses/#SmallProfits. To fit into an overall country rating, industries or groups of companies should be ranked by each of the four measures. The summed countries, industries or groups of companies rank divided by four then represents the level of earnings management.

3.6 Summary: Most Suitable Detection Techniques

This chapter provided an overview of earnings management detection techniques. The emphasis was placed on statistical procedures because they are suitable for analysis of

[46] See section 2.1.2.3 for the other earnings smoothing indicators.

Jones model and the performance matched Jones model are therefore better alternatives for the relatively small sample estimations.

Researchers concerned with questions such as how a certain accounting standard mitigates real cash flow manipulations or under which conditions managers substitute 'cheap' accrual management with the more costly real cash flow management, should use real cash flow models. However, the number of real cash flow models is limited, and they do not try to model aggregated cash flow management. A single exception is Roychowdhury (2004). Additional models are needed in this field of accounting research.

If a researcher is concerned with questions like the comparison of earnings management levels between countries or a group of companies, he should employ models that detect the aggregate affect of real cash flow and accrual manipulations. Depending on a research design both distributional tests and rankings can be used to detect earnings management. Distributional tests 'visualise' the effect of multiple earnings management motivations (e.g., to manage earnings above a certain threshold or to manage taxes[47]) on the realisations of earnings. The level of, e.g., loss avoidance can then be compared between certain groups. Ranking procedures can answer more general research questions. They aggregate in a single test motivations to smooth earnings, to boost or to decrease earnings and to avoid reporting unfavourable income numbers (recall that Leuz et al. (2003) use also a Burgstahler/Dichev (1997) distributional tests as an element of there analysis).

Empirical analysis in the chapter 4 will use some of the models described here. The concern of the first empirical analysis is the extent of accrual management. The auxiliary model that will be employed is the cash flow Jones model. Additional tests will be performed using some rankings' ratios. The second analysis is concerned with the extent of earnings management for tax purposes. The model design will employ distributional tests that (by an appropriate scaling) may trace accrual management, real cash flow management and fraud accounting.

[47] Section 4.5.3 will show how distributional tests may be employed to detect the tax evasion.

4 DETERMINANTS OF EARNINGS MANAGEMENT DECISIONS

4.1 MOTIVATIONS FOR EARNINGS MANAGEMENT

This chapter will give an overview of empirical evidence on determinants of earnings management. First, motivations for earnings management will be discussed. The chapter will provide examples of empirical research that tried to isolate certain motivations for earnings management and to show their incremental effect on reporting practices. The discussion on the motivations for earnings management will be followed by an analysis of environmental factors that may inhibit the level of income manipulation. The overview of earnings management motivations and constraints is important for two reasons: (1) to summarize the results of the empirical research, which could be interesting to the users of financial statements and the law makers, and (2) to identify gaps in this field of accounting research. This overview will be followed by the two empirical analyses, which will close some of these gaps.

The second chapter showed that the intent to manipulate accounts is crucial for earnings management. Recall that it is hard to discriminate certain legitimate accrual choices from earnings management. The presence of intent to alter reporting performance is what distinguishes income manipulation. Currently there exists a large body of empirical evidence on motivations for earnings management. Results of these studies are of immense importance to investors, standard setters and regulative authorities. Direct actions can be taken to inhibit earnings management practices once it is clear under what conditions earnings management occurs. For example, knowing that managers with an involvement in a venture that goes public may increase reported earnings via accrual management can make such companies to a target group for a more close examination by a stock market supervisor.

Not only the motivations for earnings management are, however, important. The extent of earnings management is influenced by the environment in which a firm operates. On one hand, the environment may create conditions for the increase of earnings management practices. On the other hand, an environment may positively influence the incentives to provide financial information of high quality and thus constrain income manipulation. The discussion on the motivations for earnings management will be followed by a review of an empirical evidence of the environmental settings that may inhibit earnings management practices. The section will address the influence of the demand and supply for accounting information on reporting practices. This field of empirical research is relatively new (especially in the case of the demand side). The first empirical evidence on the influence of the demand for accounting information was presented in the accounting literature in the end of 1990s and can be attributed to the studies of Ball et al. published in 2000 and 2003. Little empirical evidence exists in this field of research. Studies mostly discuss an impact of environmental forces on reporting practices using other earnings quality concepts (e.g., timeliness and conservatism) than earnings management. The evidence in these studies suggests that an increasing demand (or constraints on supply) for accounting information pushes firms to supply high quality earnings. As the results of earnings quality studies are expected to hold for earnings management, this section will fill the lack of empirical evidence on earnings management with the evidence on earnings quality.

The literature on earnings management documents a general behaviour to manage reported earnings. However it is a matter of research design to find out what exactly motivates companies to manage earnings. According to Jensen/Meckling (1976) a company can be viewed as a nexus of contracts. These contracts can be of explicit and implicit nature. Few examples of explicit contracts include incentive compensation plans and debt covenants. Implicit contracts have no legal standing. Examples are expectations of employees (e.g., working conditions and future prospects), customers (e.g., quality of provided services and continuing supply of products) and suppliers (e.g., timely payment of invoices and continuing demand for product). This view can be extended to the financial reporting context. While the explicit contracts are bound to the reported income numbers by their nature, the relation between implicit contracts and financial numbers is not straightforward. Cornell/Shapiro (1987) and Maksimovic/Titman (1991) show that the financial image of a company is important to stakeholders that have implicit claims to the company, because a company's incentives to fulfil implicit obligations are a function of its financial health. The purpose of opportunistic earnings management is to deceive contracting parties by hiding true firm performance. Empirical research provides evidence that all company's contractual parties can be victims of such actions. A few examples are: (1) creditors that provide debt according to some accounting based covenants (explicit contract) may be deceived about the true risk of their lending by income-increasing earnings management (DeFond/Jiambalvo, 1994); (2) current shareholders that pay too much on incentive compensation plans (explicit contract) because of the income-increasing earnings management (Healy, 1985); and (3) current shareholders that employ managers for a longer time (implicit contract) because the latter artificially show a good performance (DeFond/Park, 1997).

Recent research on motivations for earnings management found several groups of incentives for earnings management, e.g., capital market motivations and contractual motivations (e.g., Healy/Wahlen, 1999; Fields et al., 2001). To stay consistent with the extant literature, this chapter will classify motivations for earnings management not from the viewpoint of victims but from the viewpoint of the winning parties of discretionary decisions: managers and current shareholders. *Figure 5* shows this classification and links it to prior research by Fields et al. (2001).

The following sections will discuss only motivations for opportunistic earnings management. Signalling, however, can also be classified according to a scheme provided in *Figure 5.* From the viewpoint of shareholders earnings that convey managers' private information is a better measure for valuation and monitoring. Signalling may be also beneficial for management. Recall that it is hard to smooth earnings (i.e. to signal information on permanent earnings). Showing the ability to smooth earnings in anticipation of future income helps managers to demonstrate their predictive abilities. Thus, managers may manipulate earnings to communicate acquired expertise (Demski, 1998).

Figure 5: Motivations for earnings management

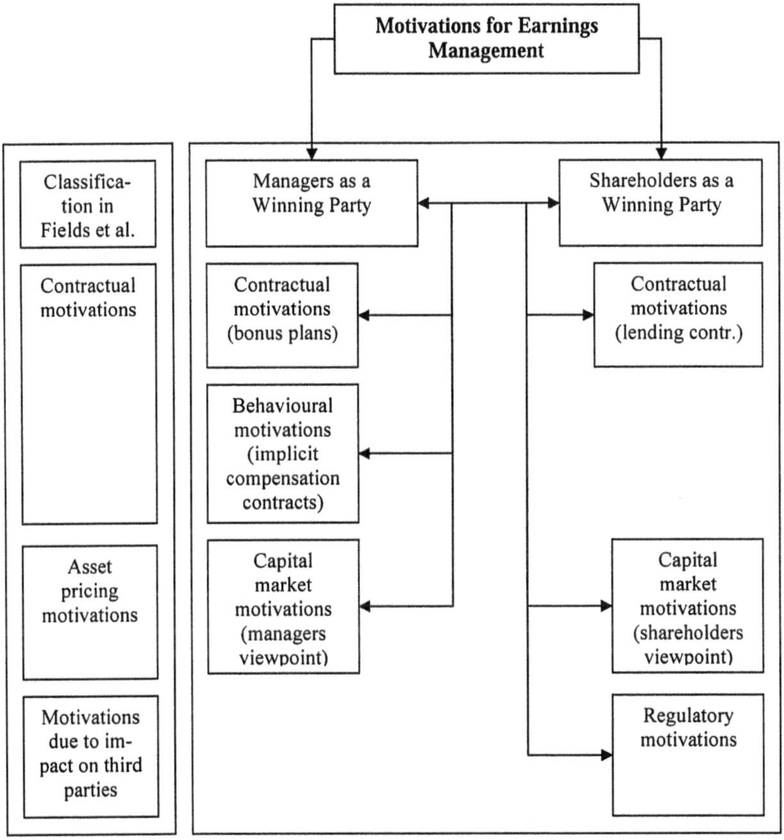

The first motivation of earnings management is to maximize the interests of current shareholders (i.e. shareholders are the winning party of earnings management), which may occur at the expense of some other contracting party (Francis, 2001, p. 312). The literature shows that managers manipulate earnings because of:

- capital market motivations, i.e. intention to avoid a drop in share price (and/or to get priced with a higher premium) by meeting/beating a target (e.g., Burgstahler/Dichev, 1997; Degeorge et al., 1999) or increase share price before a stock transaction (e.g. Teoh et al., 1998a, 1998b and 1998c; Dechow et al., 1996; Erickson/Wang, 1999);

- contractual motivations, i.e. to obtain a bank debt (Coppens/Peek, 2004) or to reduce the likelihood of a bond covenant violation (Smith/Warner, 1979; Sweeney, 1994; DeFond/Jiambalvo, 1994);[48]

- regulatory motivations, i.e. to reduce political costs (e.g., Jones, 1991; Cahan, 1992; Navissi, 1999) or to decrease the present value of taxes (Scholes et al., 1992; Cushing/LeClere, 1992; Keating/Zimmerman, 2000).

The second motivation for earnings management is managerial self-interest or opportunistic behaviour. Managerial self-interest derives for example from:

- behavioural motivations, i.e. reputation (e.g., Strong/Meyer, 1987; Elliott/Shaw, 1988; Pourciau, 1993; Murphy/Zimmerman, 1993; Wells, 2002) and job security (DeFond/Park, 1997);

- contractual motivations, i.e. short-term bonus contracts which are tied to reported accounting performance measures (Healy, 1985; Dechow/Sloan, 1991; Holthausen et al., 1995; Koch/Wall, 2000);

- capital market motivations, i.e. to decrease share price before going private (DeAngelo, 1986; Perry/Williams, 1994) or increase share prices before a hostile takeover (Easterwood, 1997/1998).

All motivations are closely related to each other. It is likely that not a single motivation but rather a set of multiple motivations drives accounting choice (Fields et al., 2001). For instance, opportunism of a company's management driven by the willingness to benefit from a bonus scheme will also lead to an increase in share prices and/or will reduce the likelihood of debt covenant violation and, therefore, not only managers but also current shareholders will profit from such behaviour. The same notion can be found in Christie/Zimmerman (1994, p. 539): "...many of the empirical regularities interpreted as evidence of opportunism can also be interpreted as occurring for effi-

[48] These are the contractual motivations from the (explicit) lending contracts. Kasanen et al. (1996) show that the implicit contracts with the firms' shareholders may also affect accounting choices. Authors use the sample of firms listed on the Helsinki Stock Exchange. Their evidence suggests that in a debt-dominated capital market with concentrated cross-ownership firms manage earnings in a way to pay out the smooth dividend stream expected by the large institutional owners.

ciency reasons". The following sections will present results of the studies that tried by research design to trace the impact of a single motivation on earnings management (often simply ignoring the presence of possibly competing incentives). Results of this research should be taken with caution because they may suffer from a correlated omitted variable problem (as only one motivation is studied at a time). Several empirical studies tried to address the influence of a set of motivations (e.g., Hand/Skantz, 1998; Francis et al., 1996). The evidence of these studies is consistent with multiple motivations driving accounting choices. Further research is needed to provide robust evidence on the interplay of different (competing) motivations (Fields et al., 2001).

4.1.1 Shareholders as a Winning Party of Earnings Management

4.1.1.1 Capital Market Motivations from the Shareholders' Viewpoint

Investors using of accounting information for valuation purposes creates incentives to manage reported earnings to influence investors' perception of the firm's performance. Incentives to affect the short term stock price performance via manipulation of earnings numbers are referred to as capital market motivations for earnings management (e.g., Healy/Wahlen, 1999). Section 2.2.2 showed that there is no consensus in empirical research on whether earnings management affects resource allocation. If markets are inefficient investors will be fooled by earnings management and will falsely react to earnings announcements. In the case of income-increasing (income-decreasing), earnings management will lead to an increase (decrease) in the short-term stock price performance. Thus, managers that want to influence share prices in inefficient stock markets have an incentive to alter firm's reported earnings.

In efficient markets it seems at first glance counterintuitive to manage earnings to affect share prices. Why would managers manipulate earnings if investors are aware of such behaviour (and its impact on current and future periods' earnings) and will rationally adjust the stock price for it? Erickson/Wang (1999) and Shivakumar (2000) provide examples of capital market motivations for earnings management in an efficient market. Shivakumar (2000) discusses earnings management behaviour preceding public offerings. He argues that management does not attempt to mislead investors by overstating earnings. Investors anticipate income-increasing adjustments by all issuers prior to an offering (as 'good' firms do not have an instrument to signal the 'truthfulness' of their earnings) and correct their stock price for such adjustments. As a response to the investors' reaction, firms rationally overstate earnings. Erickson/Wang (1999) provide another example for capital market motivations in an efficient market. In their opinion an acquirer may overstate earnings before a stock for stock merger because the target firm anticipates and prices such behaviour when negotiating a merger agreement.

To trace the presence of capital market motivations researchers tried to isolate situations in which incentives to manage earnings for capital market purposes are relatively high. Two types of scenarios were analysed empirically: company's earnings fall below a target such as zero earnings level or analyst forecasts (e.g., Burgstahler/Dichev, 1997) and stock transactions, i.e. security offerings and stock for stock mergers (e.g., Teoh et al., 1998a; Erickson/Wang, 1999).

Beating a certain earnings threshold is of immense importance for security prices. Anecdotal and empirical evidence suggest that consequent reporting of earnings above a threshold increases firm value and failing to meet a threshold disproportionately decreases firm value. A good example is Cisco Systems. Cisco reported slightly positive earnings surprises for 14 quarters and then failed to meet an analyst forecast of earnings per share by one U.S.-cent. This negative earnings surprise deflated Cisco's stock price by 13% on the day after the announcement (Collingwood, 2001). Recent empirical research also found support for the argument that stock prices are sensitive to earnings benchmarks. Barth et al. (1999) document that stocks of firms reporting consequent earnings increases are priced with a higher premium and that this premium is reduced when an earnings decline occurs. Skinner/Sloan (2000) show that stock price reactions to negative earnings surprises are disproportionately large for growth stocks. Such stock reactions illustrate the importance of meeting or beating the expectations of stock market participants and provide incentives for earnings management. Several studies analysed the presence of threshold oriented earnings management. Results of these studies are consistent with earnings management to meet a zero earnings target (Burgstahler/Dichev, 1997), to avoid an earnings decline (Burgstahler/Dichev, 1997), to beat an analyst forecast (Degeorge et al., 1999) and to beat a management earnings forecast (Kasznik, 1999).

Another line of research analysed earnings management behaviour before stock transactions. Stock transactions such as IPOs, SEOs and stock for stock mergers provide incentives to increase earnings and benefit from the enhanced short-term stock performance. Teoh et al. (1998b, 1998c) provide evidence on income-increasing earnings management during the year of an IPO. They also document that discretionary accruals during the IPO explain a poor earnings and stock performance in subsequent years. Teoh et al. (1998a) and Rangan (1998) support these findings by showing that firms manage earnings around SEOs. Dechow et al. (1996) also point to the fact that firms subject to SEC enforcement actions frequently make SEOs. Erickson/Wang (1999) investigate whether acquirers manage earnings upwards before a stock for stock merger. Stock for stock mergers provide incentives to increase the pre-merger share price of the acquiring firm: The higher the price of an acquirer's shares, the fewer shares must be issued to buy a target firm, thus reducing the merger costs. The findings of Erickson/Wang (1999) support the prediction of income-increasing earnings management to boost share prices and indicate that the extent of earnings management is correlated with the relative size of the merger.

4.1.1.2 CONTRACTUAL MOTIVATIONS: THE CASE OF LENDING CONTRACTS

Lending contracts provide motivations for earnings management in two ways: Before debt is granted companies may use earnings management to facilitate financing. Once the debt is granted firms are likely to use income-increasing earnings management to avoid a technical default.

Companies may manage earnings to obtain financing. Coppens/Peek (2004) and Burgstahler et al. (2004) discuss (but do not test empirically) incentives for earnings management of private firms. They argue that private companies have an incentive to mange earnings above the zero earnings target to facilitate the bank debt granting process. The interest on bank debt is shown in the company's income statement as interest expense and reduces a period's earnings. When a company granted with a bank credit reports accounting losses, it is not able to pay out all the fixed claims incurred. If banks believe that losses are persistent then they perceive a risk that companies showing losses will not be able to pay their interest. Therefore, the value banks attach to (positive) earnings and losses is different. This leads to a bounded value function of banks: The function is zero when the company reports a profit (as banks do not participate in the distribution of the bottom line earnings) and is bounded below at the value of the fixed claim (i.e. the interest) when a company reports a loss. The nature of fixed claims makes banks reference-dependent to a zero earnings target when estimating the financial health of the borrower. Consequently bank debt agreements may provide motivations for earnings management. Before obtaining a bank debt firms may facilitate the debt-granting process by reporting positive income numbers via earnings management.

After the debt is granted firms may employ income-increasing accounting policies to avoid debt covenant violations. According to the agency literature, the acquired debt financing can be expropriated by the entrepreneur by paying out a dividend, by issuing additional and more senior claims and/or by taking more risky projects (Smith/Warner, 1979). To protect themselves lenders employ debt contracts. These contracts usually indicate some covenants linked to a firm's accounting performance. Watts/Zimmerman (1978) argue that such contracts may provide incentives for earnings management. This was a theoretical background for the tests of earnings management to avoid the debt covenant violations or tests of the so called 'debt hypothesis'. Early research found, however, little evidence in support for the debt hypothesis. Holthausen (1981), Healy/Palepu (1990), DeAngelo et al. (1994) and Sweeney (1994) examined accounting practices of firms that are close to their dividend constraint (the first three studies) or have violated the debt covenant (the last study). All studies found little support for the effects of debt contracting on accounting choice. The only early study that found strong support for the debt hypothesis was the work by DeFond/Jiambalvo (1994). The authors used a sample of firms that reported a debt covenant violation. They show that the abnormal accruals in the year preceding the covenant violation and in the year of covenant violation are significantly positive, which is consistent with the debt hypothesis.

One of the major limitations of these studies is the selection bias (Fields et al., 2001). Analysed companies are either close to debt covenant violation or have already violated covenants, i.e. researchers fail to account for successful attempts to avoid a covenant violation, which induces selection bias. Recent studies by Beatty/Weber (2003) and Dichev/Skinner (2002) resolve this problem and provide evidence consistent with the debt hypothesis. Dichev/Skinner (2002) use a distribution of the variable labelled "covenant slack" that equals the difference between firm's accounting measure and relevant covenant threshold on private borrowing. The presence of the discontinuity around zero in the histograms of this variable is consistent with the debt hypothesis. Beatty/Weber (2003) show that the following types of firms are more likely to make income-increasing accounting method changes: (1) the firms with debt contracts allowing accounting changes affect covenant calculation; (2) firms having only one lender; (3) firms having borrowing contracts allowing accounting changes affect covenant calculation and performance-pricing provisions in the debt contracts (i.e. accounting measures affect not only the likelihood of the debt covenant violation but also the interest rate of the borrowing); and (4) firms having borrowing contracts allowing accounting changes affect covenant calculation and dividend restrictions. Their results are robust to the presence of correlated motivations to increase earnings (e.g., management compensation and taxes). This evidence is also consistent with the debt hypothesis.

4.1.1.3 Regulatory Motivations

Regulatory motivations for earnings management gained much attention in the academic literature in the late 1970s. The insights of Watts and Zimmerman into explanation and prediction of accounting practices provided a theoretical background for research on a so called 'political cost hypothesis' (Watts/Zimmermann, 1978 and 1979). In the core of this hypothesis there is the notion that "the political sector has the power to effect wealth transfers between various groups" (Watts/Zimmerman, 1978, p. 115). The political sector may affect firms' prosperity because firms are subjects of potential wealth transfer initiated by the state. Wealth transfer can be a result of either a regulatory action (e.g., antitrust investigations, damage awards, import relief investigations) or a tax claim. According to the political cost hypothesis firms will adapt accounting policies that will minimize the likelihood (the magnitude) of the wealth transfer from them to other parties.

Early empirical research on the political cost hypothesis used very noisy proxies to test the presence of regulatory motivations for accrual choices. Some authors used firm size (e.g., Moyer, 1990; Scott, 1991), profit margin (Sutton, 1988), tax rates and export credit sales (Zimmerman, 1983; Wong, 1988) as measures for firm's vulnerability to political costs. According to the theory large earnings can make a firm more visible to a regulator and can be used to justify political actions against the firm's interests because of "the public's association of high reported profits and monopoly rents" (Watts/Zimmermann, 1978, p. 115). Consistently, firm size is expected to be positively correlated with income-decreasing accounting choices aimed to reduce the likelihood of the wealth transfer against firm's interests. However, researchers found little support for this prediction: While e.g., Lilien/Pastena (1982), Daley/Vigeland (1983) and Sutton (1998) show evidence consistent with income-decreasing accrual choices of large firms, e.g., Johnson/Ramanan (1988), Wong (1988), Moyer (1990) and Scott (1991) present results inconsistent with the political cost hypothesis.

Table 4: Regulatory actions and earnings management

Type of regulatory action	Author	Firm action
Import relief investigations (i.e. general escape clause investigations, antidumping investigations and countervailing duty investigations)	Jones (1991) Magnan et al. (1999)	Income-decreasing earnings management
Antitrust investigations	Cahan (1992) Makar et al. (1998)	Income-decreasing earnings management
Litigation events (damage awards)	Hall/Stammerjohan (1997 and 2003)	Income-decreasing earnings management
Price regulation	Navissi (1999)	Income-decreasing earnings management
Political scrutiny/oversight (with potential regulation)	Key (1997) Han/Wang (1998) Beekes (2003)	Income-decreasing earnings management
	Gaver/Paterson (2004)	Income-increasing earnings management

Further research tried to overcome difficulties related to the noisy proxies for political costs by a different research design. Research concentrated on samples of companies subject to a specific regulatory action, e.g. anti-trust investigation. A necessary feature of the research design is the use of accounting data during governmental inquiry. Only explicit use of accounting measures such as raw earnings or some profitability metrics by investigators may provide incentives for managers to alter the results of financial performance.[49] Evidence in these studies is consistent with regulatory motivations affect firms' accrual choices (e.g., Jones, 1991; Key 1997). Two sets of scenarios were addressed empirically: (1) a situation in which companies try to induce a positive regulatory action (e.g., Jones, 1991; Navissi, 1999), and (2) a situation in which companies try to avoid a negative regulatory action (e.g., Cahan, 1992; Makar et al., 1998). *Table 4* shows examples of regulatory actions that were the drivers of earnings management.

Taxes represent the second mechanism by which wealth can be transferred from the firm. Earnings management for tax purposes has been widely discussed in the literature and is related to a reduction of the present value of income tax expense. Empirical research documented a general tendency of companies to manage taxes. Kasanen et al. (1996) report results consistent with earnings management to reduce taxes by Finnish listed firms. Cushing/LeClere (1992) and Keating/Zimmerman (2000) show that tax concerns affect firms' policy choices for inventory accounting and depreciation.

A significant body of research on earnings management for tax purposes considered the impact of the 1986 Tax Reform Act (TRA 1986) in United States on the income shifting behaviour of companies. A known schedule of declining tax rates from 46% to 34% for the period of two years provided incentives for the firms to manage earnings in a way that would bring tax benefits from the differences in the statutory tax rate before and after the Tax Act was passed. Empirical evidence in Scholes et al. (1992) suggests that firms shifted income through deferrals of sales and acceleration of expenses to the periods with the lower statutory tax rate. Maydew (1997) shows that the firms increased net operating losses carrybacks in the period after TRA 1986 to achieve the tax savings in the amount of income shifted times statutory tax rate difference. A number of researchers studied the consequences of TRA 1986 adoption on accrual decisions of the firms and found results consistent with earnings management to reduce present value of taxes (see Boynton et al. (1992) and Gramlich (1991) in respect to aggregate discretionary accruals; Guenther (1994) in respect to current discretionary accruals; Manzon (1992) in respect to depreciation, depletion and amortization expense; Wang (1994) in respect to changes in accounting estimates).

4.1.2 Managers as a Winning Party of Earnings Management

4.1.2.1 Capital Market Motivations from the Management's Viewpoint

Not only shareholders are a winning party of capital market oriented earnings management but also managers. Discretionary increases in earnings before an IPO or when earnings would otherwise fall bellow a certain target will be beneficial for sharehold-

[49] Regulators are also hypothesized to have weak incentives and knowledge to undo earnings management.

ers and managers as well: Current shareholders can profit from the (short-term) increase in firm value; managers can benefit from compensation linked to stock performance. However, there are also situations in which managers can directly benefit from capital market oriented earnings management. Managers may decrease earnings before management buyouts ("going private") or increase earnings when the company is a takeover target.

Management buyouts (MBOs) of public stockholders were studied by DeAngelo (1986) and Perry/Williams (1994). MBOs provide a unique opportunity to study earnings management. For at least two reasons managers of firms that go private have strong incentives to manage earnings downwards. First, managing earnings downwards may reduce the stock price and make the buyout cheaper. Second, lower earnings may justify the fairness of the buyout price proposed to shareholders. DeAngelo (1986) was the first to analyse earnings management behaviour preceding MBOs. By analysing the change in accruals she finds little support for income-decreasing earnings management. In the following study Perry/Williams (1994) used a sample that is almost three times larger than DeAngelo's sample and a more sophisticated discretionary accruals model (residuals from the Jones (1991) model are used to proxy for earnings management). Their results are consistent with income-decreasing earnings management by firms that go private.

Takeover contests is another situation where incentives to manage earnings are relatively high. Evidence suggests that managers of the firms that were a takeover target often lose control over the firm after the takeover (e.g., Walking/Long, 1984). To keep the benefits of control, managers of target firms may increase reported earnings to enhance the stock performance and discourage the bidder.[50] Easterwood (1997/1998) tests this hypothesis by analysing a sample of 110 firms that were takeover targets. Her results are consistent with managers of target firms making income-increasing accruals to boost stock prices. Further splitting the sample into hostile and friendly takeovers, Easterwood shows that his results are mostly driven by hostile takeover targets.

4.1.2.2 Contractual Motivations: The Case of Explicit Compensation Contracts

Section 4.1.1.2 discussed the possible agency conflicts between shareholders and debtholders. Yet the attempts to solve another type of agency conflict – a conflict between the agent (manager) and the principal (shareholder) – may also trigger earnings management. According to the agency theory, this problem arises due to the separation of

[50] An alternative explanation is that by showing higher profits managers try to convince current shareholders that they are good performers. This may reduce the likelihood that current shareholders will tender their shares (Easterwood, 1997/1998).

ownership and control. It was first addressed by Berle/Means (1932) and later formalized by e.g., Jensen/Meckling (Jensen/Meckling, 1976; Fama/Jensen, 1983a; Fama/Jensen, 1983b; Jensen, 1986; Jensen et al., 1992; Jensen, 1993). The core of this problem is the informational asymmetry between owners (shareholders) and their agents (managers). Every individual is interested in maximising his own utility and managers may take actions which can violate the interest of shareholders. "The basic agency problem resulting from the separation of management and financing is that the managers will have incentives to take actions to increase their own utility, but not to maximise the returns on capital invested by financiers" (Sloan, 2001, p. 340). An opportunistic agent may use provided funds (the principal's investment) in a way to maximize his own benefit instead of maximizing shareholders' returns (Jensen/Meckling, 1976). An agent may expropriate the principal's cash to pay out excessive compensation, take on risky or harmful investment projects (e.g., 'empire building' behaviour). To align the interests of managers and shareholders agency theory proposes to use contracts – incentive compensation plans that are linked to net income, ROA and ROE for short-term incentive compensation and stock performance for the long-term incentive compensation. As in the case of the lending contracts (debt covenants), bonus contracts may also provide motivations for earnings management, which are expected to be especially strong for earnings-based compensation agreements. Commonly in (earnings-based) compensation contracts four factors are present: (1) a variant of reported earnings, (2) a lower bound or target, (3) a upper limit or cap and (4) a maximum percentage of the excess of earnings over the target that can be allocated to a bonus pool. The lower bound equals the amount of the accounting number needed to be reached to obtain bonus compensation. The upper limit is the maximum amount of the excess of earnings over the target. Seminally, Healy (1985) predicted opportunistic behaviour of managers granted with incentive compensation contracts. If unmanaged earnings fall either below the lower bound or above the upper limit of the bonus contract, managers will select income-decreasing accruals to shift earnings into future period(s), thus increasing the intertemporal remuneration. Income increasing behaviour is then used in other cases to increase the current period bonus plan remuneration.

Empirical research found support for the 'bonus plan hypothesis'. Healy (1985) reports income-decreasing behaviour for firm-years with earnings far below the lower bound or over the upper limit and income-increasing behaviour for the other firm-years (i.e. total accruals in the first two groups are significantly lower than total accruals in the third group). Holthausen et al. (1995) using a more sophisticated performance-based discretionary accruals model and confidential data of the executive-specific short-term bonus plan replicate Healy's results for the upper limit but fail to do so for the lower bound. Despite the absence of evidence for the lower bound, the authors claim that their results are consistent with the bonus plan hypothesis. They argue that job anxiety and/or other contracts bound to the reported income numbers (e.g., debt covenants) may influence managers' behaviour when earnings fall short of the bonus target: Managers of poorly performing firms will not decrease earnings if such behaviour increases the likelihood that they will be fired or will violate a debt covenant. Guidry et al. (1999) find further support for the Healy's predictions using a sample of business unit-level short-term bonus plan data. By using unit-level data, the authors avoid an aggregation bias and competing incentives induced by the long-term performance plans present in Healy (1985) and Holthausen et al. (1995). Guidry et al. (1999) find strong evidence for the income-decreasing earnings management at the lower and upper limits.

4.1.2.3 Behavioural Motivations: Implicit Compensation Contracts

Two types of behavioural motivations for earnings management were empirically addressed by accounting researchers: a wish to show a better performance than the former CEO and job anxiety. A number of studies analysed earnings management during CEO changes (e.g., Strong/Meyer, 1987; Elliott/Shaw, 1988; Pourciau, 1993; Murphy/Zimmerman, 1993; Wells, 2002). These studies predict that the incoming CEO will decrease reported earnings (e.g., via operating decisions such as research and development expenditures and accruals) during the transition year and increase earnings in the subsequent periods. The purpose of such behaviour is to maximize the compensation level in explicit and implicit contracts. Maximization of explicit compensation is consistent with contractual motivations for earnings management discussed in the previous section. Firm performance during the first (partial) year after an executive change is unimportant for an incoming CEO: Explicit compensation contracts of incoming executives are bound to the figures of successive years. An incoming CEO is expected to take an 'earnings bath' to shift earnings to future periods thus increasing his overall bonus-based compensation. Evidence in the studies on CEO changes provides, therefore, additional support for the bonus plan hypothesis.

Motivations for earnings management surrounding CEO changes may also exist in the absence of explicit bonus contracts (Wells, 2002). As manager's performance is assessed regularly, earnings management may be also driven by implicit contracts. Showing good performance (relative to the benchmark of the previous CEO performance) positively influences the manager's reputation and may cause an ex-post renegotiation of his remuneration. According to this scenario, the incoming CEO will blame the incumbent for a poor firm performance during the transition year. Reversal of discretionary accruals in subsequent years will 'justify' his (i.e. the incoming CEO's) opinion.

Results of the studies on earnings management surrounding CEO changes show evidence consistent with incoming CEOs managing earnings downwards. Strong/Meyer (1987), Elliott/Shaw (1988) and Francis et al. (1996) analyse the determinants of discretionary asset writedowns. Evidence in these studies indicates that incoming managers are likely to 'clear the decks' via assets writedowns to enhance an opportunity to show better firm performance in future periods. Pourciau (1993) and Murphy/Zimmerman (1993) address the role of accruals in earnings management surrounding CEO changes. Both studies find (weak) evidence for income-decreasing earnings management by the incoming CEO.

Not only the desire to be better than the leaving CEO may drive earnings management. Fudenberg/Tirole (1995) argue that concerns about job security drive income-increasing (income-decreasing) choices during the bad (good) years (i.e. income smoothing). During the bad years managers are expected to boost earnings to reduce the likelihood of dismissal. During good years managers may 'save' income for future periods to lengthen their tenure. DeFond/Park (1997) build on this theory and provide evidence on income smoothing in anticipation of future earnings.

4.2 EARNINGS MANAGEMENT CONSTRAINTS

4.2.1 REPORTING PRACTICES AS A FUNCTION OF DEMAND FOR AND SUPPLY OF ACCOUNTING INFORMATION

Recent empirical research showed a tremendous importance of the reporting environment as an earnings management constraint (e.g., Ball et al. 2000; Leuz et al., 2003). Extant research suggests that accounting practices are a function of the interplay between the firm's political, social, cultural, legal, and economic environment. These factors shape reporting practices and determine greatly the extent of earnings management. The reporting environment may influence the extent of earnings management either through a demand for high quality information or through the constraints on the supply of accounting information. This section will discuss issues related to the demand for accounting information. Subsequent sections will address supply-side constraints of earnings management: political forces, governance structures, culture, auditing and accounting standards. While the sections will discuss the incremental effect of certain environmental factors, the extent of earnings quality (or earnings management) is likely to be determined by the interplay between these factors. A set of factors rather than a single one constrains earnings management.

Ball et al. (2003, p. 236) argue that the preparer's incentives to supply earnings of a high quality depend on market forces. The extent of their influence depends on the relationship between managers and the stockholders, and importance of the stock market (i.e. the number of listed companies or the market size). In countries with developed capital markets and dispersed ownership, market forces push firms to report high quality earnings. Shareholders in such countries are obliged to use the publicly available financial information for valuation purposes and monitoring of the company's activities. According to the theory investors are not willing to trade in shares of firms that report accounting data of low quality, which is not suitable for valuation and/or monitoring. They thus increase the illiquidity component of a firm's cost of capital. By otherwise demanding a higher cost of capital, investors push firms to supply accounting information of a higher quality (e.g., Burgstahler et al., 2004).

To shed more light on the influence of market forces on earnings quality empirical research concentrated on the differences between common-law and code-law countries and between private and public firms. In the common-law countries (e.g., U.S. and U.K.) only the general principles are enacted by the government. Courts interpret these general principles to build a body of case law. Such countries are characterized by large, developed capital markets with shares of companies belonging to a vast number of shareholders. Financial statements in this case are the major source of information for investors. To raise additional capital at a low price companies have to supply high quality accounting information. In the code-law countries (e.g., Germany and France) the demand for accounting information was traditionally low. These countries are characterized by less developed capital markets and concentrated ownership structures (which is changing since the beginning of 1990s). Information is rather communicated through private channels. Such reduced demand for accounting information negatively affects incentives to supply earnings of a high quality. Ball et al. (2000) provide empirical evidence on the influence of the demand for accounting information on the properties of earnings in the code- and common-law countries. The authors conclude that earnings in common-law countries have a superior quality (in terms of timeliness and conservatism). The problem of such kind of studies, however, is their research design. The market forces vary between the countries, as do the accounting standards. In such empirical design one cannot clearly isolate the effect of the standards (Holthausen, 2003).

To further understand the incremental effect of market forces, researchers began to concentrate on the differences in reporting practices between firms reporting under one set of accounting standards. Studies on the differences of earnings quality between private and public firms provide stronger support for the importance of reporting incentives. An appealing feature of the research design in such studies is that companies are usually studied under one reporting jurisdiction (i.e. domiciled in one country): Private and public companies report using the same set of accounting rules. The differences in reporting practices can be more easily attributed to the different demand for accounting information of the two groups of companies. Private firms usually have a concentrated ownership. There is no need for them to communicate information on company's performance via financial statements. Private firm's performance is assessed through private communication rather than through the analysis of accounting information. Evidence on the differences in the levels of earnings quality between private and public firms is documented in Ball/Shivakumar (forthcoming) and Burgstahler et al. (2004). Ball/Shivakumar (forthcoming) compare the quality of earnings of private and public firms in the U.K. The authors show that losses of private companies are not incorporated on a timely basis because there is no demand for high quality information of private firms. Burgstahler et al. (2004) show that the level of earnings management is higher for private European firms as for their counterparts with a stock exchange listing.

4.2.2 Supply-side Constraints

4.2.2.1 Political Forces

Political forces influence reporting practices either directly through the laws e.g., on accounting, taxes, investor protection and their enforcement (Ball et al., 2000 and 2003) or indirectly through the interplay with market forces. La Porta et al. (1998) explain how political forces may influence the market forces:

> "The rights attached to securities become critical when managers of companies act in their own interest. These rights give investors the power to extract from managers the returns on their investment. Shareholders receive dividends because they can vote out the directors who do not pay them, and creditors are paid because they have the power to repossess collateral. … Law and the quality of its enforcement are potentially important determinants of what rights security holders have and how well these rights are protected. Since the protection investors receive determines the readiness to finance firms, corporate finance may critically turn on these legal rules and their enforcement." (La Porta et al., 1998, p. 1114)

Laws on investor protection and the extent of their enforcement may influence the demand for accounting information and through it the quality of reported earnings. The current section will address only the issues related to the direct influence of political forces.

Investment in the firm' equity capital bears the risk that the invested funds and the returns on them will be expropriated by the insiders, i.e. controlling shareholders and managers (La Porta et al., 2000). Expropriation can take a number of forms: "in some instances, insiders simply steal the profits. In other instances, the insiders sell the output, the assets, or the additional securities in the firm they control to another firm they own at below market prices… In still other cases, expropriation takes the form of diversion of corporate opportunities from the firm, installing possibly unqualified family members in managerial positions, or overpaying executives" (La Porta et al., 2000, p. 3).

In any way insiders are not interested to communicate information about expropriations to outsiders. With the help of earnings management insiders will hide their private control benefits from the outsiders, because outsiders with the knowledge of such private information would take disciplinary actions against insiders, i.e. replace the management (e.g., Zingales, 1994). The success of disciplinary actions depends to a high degree on the laws on investor protection and their enforcement. The legal system protects investors (outsiders) by: (1) providing rights to discipline insiders; (2) enforcement of the contracts that mitigate private control benefits (e.g., La Porta et al., 1998; Dyck/Zingales, 2004). An effective legal system is therefore expected to reduce the extent of earnings management.

Leuz et al. (2003) provide empirical evidence on the influence of laws on earnings quality by comparing the level of earnings management in 31 countries. Evidence in this study is consistent with the rules on investor protection influencing the magnitude of income manipulation (i.e. income smoothing and discretion in reported earnings).

Political forces may influence the extent of earnings management through the law enforcement. Empirical evidence in Leuz et al. (2003) suggests that legal enforcement reduces income manipulations. Lang et al. (2004) compare earnings quality of U.S. firms and non-U.S. firms listed in the U.S. and reporting under U.S. GAAP. They show that the lack of SEC enforcement in respect to non-U.S. firms results in non-U.S. companies' earnings being of a lower quality.

4.2.2.2 CULTURE

One (of many) definitions of culture can be found in Hofstede (1980). He describes culture as "the collective programming of the mind which distinguishes the member of one human group from another" (Hofstede, 1980, p. 25). Accounting theory suggests that accounting values and practices depend on culture. Both the theoretical framework and the empirical evidence on the effects of culture on accounting practices began to accumulate in the recent accounting literature. Gray (1988, p. 1) argues:

> "While prior research has shown that there are different patterns of accounting internationally and that the development of national systems tends to be a function of environmental factors, it is a matter of some controversy as to the identification of the patterns and influential factors involved. ... In this context the significance of culture does not appear to have been fully appreciated and thus the purpose of this paper is to propose a framework which links culture with the development of accounting systems internationally".

There are many ways to classify culture. Hofstede (1980) shows that countries may be differentiated according to four cultural dimensions: individualism, power distance, uncertainty avoidance, and masculinity. These cultural dimensions affect accounting values which in turn affect "the structure and practice of accounting, including the basic tenets of measurement and disclosure which determine financial reporting practices" (Salter/Niswander, 1995, p. 380). Therefore, the extent of earnings management is also expected to be dependent on the cultural dimensions:

- Individualism versus collectivism: Individualism is present in societies where relations between the individuals are very loose. In this case "everybody is supposed to look after his/her own self-interest and maybe the interest of his/her immediate family" (Hofstede, 1983, p. 44). The extent of opportunistic earnings management may be higher in the individualist countries because managers in such countries will use income-increasing accruals to maximise their own interest. Collectivism on the other hand is expected to inhibit earnings management practices.

- Large versus small power distance: Power distance "reflects how society deals with inequality" (Hofstede, 1983, p. 44). In societies with a large power distance subordinates are more likely to accept hierarchical orders without requesting their justification. In such societies earnings management can be expected to be more widespread.

- Strong versus weak uncertainty avoidance: Uncertainty avoidance "concerns how society deals with the fact that time runs only one direction" (Hofstede, 1983, p. 44). In the countries with a high uncertainty avoidance individuals have a higher level of anxiety, are more nervous and aggressive. Societies feeling more uncomfortable with uncertainty create different types of institutions to provide a feeling of security. In such societies managers are expected to take income-decreasing (income-increasing) accruals in good (bad) years to smooth earnings.

- Masculinity versus femininity: Masculinity "stands for a preference in society for achievement, heroism, assertiveness, and material success" (Gray, 1988, p. 10). The goal achievement behaviour is positively related to non-conservative accounting and should be a driver of aggressive earnings management. A desire to beat an earnings threshold (e.g., the zero earnings level or analyst forecasts) may be also higher in the masculine countries.

Several recent empirical studies showed that cultural values as measured by Hofstede (1980) play an important role in explaining cross-country variations in the extent of earnings management practices. Kinnunen/Koskela (2003) find that power distance is positively related to earnings management practices in 18 countries. Using different earnings management measures Guan/Pourjalali (2003) arrive at the conclusion that all four variables representing cultural values (i.e. power distance, individualism, masculinity and uncertainty avoidance) are helpful in explaining the direction and magnitude of accrual manipulations.

4.2.2.3 CORPORATE GOVERNANCE

Corporate governance can be described as "a set of mechanisms through which outside investors protect themselves against expropriation by the insiders" (La Porta et al., 2000, p. 4). A related definition is given by Shleifer/Vishny (1997, p. 737): "Corporate Governance deals with the ways in which suppliers of finance to corporations assure themselves of getting a return to their investment". According to the agency perspective the need for corporate governance arises from this separation of ownership and control: 'Good' corporate governance is supposed to prevent managers from taking actions that violate interests of the shareholders. Earnings management provides opportunities to hide true firm performance and to increase opportunistically manager's utility. 'Good' corporate governance structures are expected to constrain such opportunistic earnings management practices.

Empirical research provided evidence on the role of the following corporate governance elements on earnings management: ownership structure, board and auditing committee. Board and auditing committee are mandatory for all listed firms (at least in the U.S.). Therefore, researchers concentrated on indirect measures of efficiency of these corporate governance mechanisms.

The impact of two types of shareholdings on earnings management was analysed empirically: institutional holdings and managerial ownership. Institutional investors with big shareholdings in a firm have strong incentives to monitor firm's performance (e.g., Shleifer/Vishny, 1997). Chung et al. (2002) build on this argument and show that large institutional holdings inhibit discretionary use of accruals.

The separation of ownership and control causes potential agency costs. Managers without a significant involvement in an enterprise are predicted to behave selfishly. To reduce agency costs and to discipline managers, agents use contracts. These contracts, however, provide incentives for earnings management. The negative relation between the extent of earnings management and managerial ownership is predicted under the assumption that the opportunistic behaviour and the use of contractual constraints decrease with managerial ownership. This hypothesis is empirically supported by Warfield et al. (1995).

The board is another important corporate governance structure constructed to protect the interests of shareholders. According to Fama/Jensen (1983a) a board of directors exercises the monitoring of management activities on behalf of the shareholders. How well a board copes with this task, depends on its properties. Accounting research addressed empirically three properties of the board: board independence, financial sophistication of the board members and the number of the board meetings. Xie et al. (2003) provide evidence consistent with the importance of the board in mitigating earnings management. They show that the number of board meetings and financial backgrounds of the board members are negatively related to the extent of income manipulations. Despite the fact that outsiders on the board may not have supreme knowledge of the company's activities, they are in the position to ask questions and to hire external consultants to examine, for example, questionable accounting practices. Consistently, Klein (2002) and Peasnell et al. (2000) find that board independence is negatively related to the magnitude of discretionary accruals.

Audit committees are the last corporate governance vehicle whose relation to earnings management was assessed empirically. The audit committee should meet regularly to oversee the financial reporting process and internal accounting controls. The role of the audit committee is, inter alia, to reduce (the risk of) earnings management. Researchers found a negative relation between the extent of earnings management and the meeting frequency (Xie et al., 2003), members financial sophistication (Xie et al., 2003), and committee independence (Klein, 2002).

4.2.2.4 AUDITING

Auditing plays a very important role in inhibiting earnings management. Shareholders (may) hire auditors to resolve information asymmetries about the true economic performance of a company between them and the management. Auditors verify then the validity of financial statements and detect questionable accounting practices that may affect the wealth of shareholders. The effectiveness of auditing (i.e. the extent to which earnings management is detected) depends on the quality of the provided audit services (Becker et al, 1998).

The impact of auditing on the extent of earnings management is empirically hard to trace as all public companies have to be audited. Comparing public companies with private companies or comparing public companies in a cross-country analysis is likely to bring biased results. Audit quality varies with the reporting incentives and institutional factors in such research designs. Researchers mostly concentrated on the indirect measures of auditing quality such as auditor size (measured as Big N auditor or auditor industry expertise), auditor tenure and auditor (in)dependence (measured as the extent of provided non-auditing services). DeAngelo (1981) notes that big auditor companies have 'more to lose' if client's earnings management practices become publicly known. Empirical research provides results consistent with the auditor size (as a proxy for auditing quality) can mitigate income manipulations. Becker et al. (1998), Francis et al. (1999) and Bauwhede et al. (2003) find that Big Six auditors constrain earnings management. Krishnan (2003) supports these results by showing that industry specific auditor expertise is negatively associated with absolute discretionary accruals.

Auditor tenure is positively related to the knowledge of the firm-specific risks and negatively to audit failures. Therefore, auditor tenure may reduce the magnitude of earnings management. Myers et al. (2003) provide evidence that the magnitude of discretionary accruals decreases with the auditor tenure. This evidence is important in the light of the ongoing debate about a mandatory auditor change. Results in Myers et al. (2003) suggest that a mandatory auditor change would not lead to an increase in earnings quality as measured by the magnitude of discretionary accruals.

Another group of researchers studied the impact of non-audit services on the magnitude of earnings management. After Enron the standard setters view non-audit services provided by auditing firms as deteriorating audit quality. The fees for non-audit services are expected to be positively correlated with the extent of earnings management by auditors' clients. Empirical research, however, found little support for this argument (e.g., Antle et al., 2002; Larcker/Richardson, 2003).

4.2.2.5 Accounting Standards

In recent times earnings management has been often seen by academics and practitioners as a function of latitude in accounting standards (e.g., Levitt, 1998). The accounting standards provide different (amount of) accounting choices and therefore may supply earnings of different quality. Earnings management is expected to be more spread under lax regimes that leave sufficient space for making judgments.

While there is no doubt that accounting standards are different in respect to the amount of accounting choices they allow, researchers failed to provide clear evidence for a link between an accounting regimes' properties and the level of earnings management. There are several qualitative studies that compared accounting regimes. Usually two sets of competing accounting frameworks are compared: IAS/IFRS and U.S. GAAP, where IAS/IFRS provide a sufficient number of alternative treatments (Meitner et al., 2002, p. 140; Born, 2001b, p. 27; Müller/Wulf, 2001, p. 2206). This may be explained by the purpose of IAS/IFRS. IAS/IFRS have to be flexible enough to be applied under different national circumstances. Thus IAS/IFRS may have to provide more opportunities to entities in different countries to treat events in the most appropriate way to their respective environments. For instance, Dye/Sunder (2001, p. 265) claim that "lax IASB standards allow firms more opportunity to manage their earnings". U.S. GAAP is said to provide practically no alternatives and to be "on average more conservative than non-U.S. GAAP" (Pownall/Schipper, 1999, p. 264).

Despite theoretical evidence points to the fact that accounting standards themselves may play a substantial role in determining the extent of earnings management, it is still unclear whether the observed differences in accounting practices of entities using different accounting frameworks result actually from the allowed latitude of the accepted accounting principles. Methodologically, typical previous empirical research has isolated economic circumstances such as IPOs or specific subsets of the managerial feasible set in such a way that incentive structures could clearly be determined (see e.g.,

Teoh et al. (1998b) for IPOs; Teoh et al. (1998a) for SEOs; and Jones (1991) for import relief investigations). With this clear focus on particular events and a general limitation to one single institutional framework, the overall role of standards in earnings management has not yet been systematically addressed in such studies. The lack of a systematic analysis of accounting standards is partly due to the overall research design. It is possible to analyse the inhibiting role of accounting standards either by concentrating on the impact of certain accounting rules on reporting practices (i.e. disaggregated approach) or by analysing the aggregated relative effect of an accounting framework on the quality of reported earnings. The disaggregated approach only answers the question whether a certain accounting rule can inhibit earnings management, rather than whether one accounting regime performs better than the other. Under the aggregated approach studies on earnings management typically cover one single market to which only one set of standards applies. To inquire the relative performance of accounting regimes, it is first necessary to find a single market in which accounting regimes compete. Cross-country analyses are difficult to interpret as institutional factors vary as do the standards themselves (Holthausen, 2003). Results are therefore very likely to suffer from a severe omitted variable problem.

Using the disaggregated approach Black et al. (1998) compare the extent of real earnings management via the asset sales timing in countries with the accounting frameworks that differ according to a noncurrent assets revaluation option. The evidence of this paper is consistent with accounting rule on asset revaluation inhibiting the extent of income smoothing.

Researchers also analysed the relative quality of accounting regimes in a single market using earnings quality concepts different from earnings management. The results of these studies are mixed. Leuz (2003) and Bartov et al. (2002) using different market measures of earnings quality compare earnings under different accounting regimes of German listed companies. Leuz (2003) finds no differences in the bid-ask spreads and the share turnover between U.S. GAAP and IAS/IFRS sub-samples of firms listed on the German's Neuer Markt (New Market).[51] Bartov et al. (2002) investigate the value relevance of accounting earnings under national and international standards. They conclude that earnings are more value relevant under the international framework (i.e. IAS/IFRS or U.S. GAAP) than under German GAAP and that U.S. GAAP earnings are of a superior relevance than IAS/IFRS earnings for the sub-samples of Neuer Markt and small firms.

Studies that make cross-country comparisons of accounting standards also do not provide convergent results. Leuz et al. (2003), after controlling for endogeneity, do not find that the extent of earnings management is explained by cross-country differences in accounting rules. On the other hand Kinnunen/Koskela (2003, Table 6, p. 60) report results consistent with latitude in accounting rules explaining a sufficient proportion in

[51] Neuer Markt was a segment of the Frankfurt Stock Exchange launched in 1997 and designed for innovative and fast-growing companies.

the cross-country variations of cosmetic earnings management measures. Buijink et al. (2004) compare private companies across European countries and hypothesise that earnings of private firms in "investor-oriented" countries are on average more conservative than earnings of their counterparts in "creditor-oriented" countries. In spite the fact that private firms have homogeneous reporting incentives the authors attribute observed differences in the levels of conservatism between the groups to the remaining differences of accounting standards between European countries.

4.3 Summary and Perspectives for Future Research

Knowing under which conditions opportunistic earnings management is going to spread is crucial for its detection and prevention. More direct actions as enforcement and contracting can be taken as long as it is clear what drives income manipulations. A large body of accounting research concentrated on the determinants of earnings management. This literature can be broadly divided into studies examining motivations for earnings management and studies showing an importance of certain mechanisms that can inhibit earnings management.

The academic literature has identified numerous motivations to manage earnings. Prior research has broadly classified them into three categories: contractual motivations, asset pricing motivations and motivations due to impact on third parties. These three motivational types can be further subdivided into categories with respect to the winning party of earnings management: managers and shareholders. Early research on motivations to manage earnings found little support for the postulated hypothesis. Access to new data samples and more sophisticated models, however, shed more light on the separate impact that particular motivations have on the level of earnings management. However, the identification of additional earnings management drivers and more international evidence is still needed to build up a consistent theory of earnings management drivers. A more severe limitation of the research on motivations will be discussed later as it affects the whole research in the field of determinants of earnings management.

Recently, accounting researchers began to examine the impact of certain institutional conditions that can constrain earnings management. The demand for accounting information and constraints on the supply of accounting information determine accounting choice and may inhibit earnings management. Research on the crucial role of the demand for accounting information was heralded by Ball et al. who showed that market forces 'push' firms to report earnings of a higher quality. Earnings quality concepts that were analysed are earnings conservatism/timeliness and value relevance. Despite the fact that the results of these studies are expected to hold for earnings management, additional research on the impact of market forces on the extent of earnings management is awaited.

Supply side constraints are political forces, corporate governance, auditing, culture, and accounting standards. Researchers have shown that strong political enforcement, 'good' corporate governance, high quality auditing and certain cultural features may inhibit earnings management. Empirical literature, however, failed to provide consistent evidence of the impact of the accounting framework on the level of earnings management. Theoretical and anecdotal evidence point to the fact that accounting standards differ in respect to the amount of provided opportunities for earnings management. Every earnings management instrument has its unique costs. These costs are an increasing function of the extent to which the instrument is used to manage earnings. Limiting the number of accounting choices or defining clearer rules may increase accrual management costs and decrease the level of accrual management. Ewert/Wagenhofer (2004) support this argument by analytically modelling the economic effects of tightening accounting standards. They show that tightening "...leads to a strict decrease of accounting [i.e. accrual] earnings management because it becomes more costly to achieve a desired level of the accounting report" (Ewert/Wagenhofer, 2004, p. 17). However, the expected level of total earnings management, which incorporates both the accrual management and the "real" earnings management, can increase as managers substitute manipulation of accrual accounts by manipulation of cash flows (i.e., choosing the timing and amount of operating and investment decisions).

Several empirical studies showed results on the extent of earnings management under different accounting frameworks (Leuz et al., 2003; Kinnunen/Koskela, 2003). The intent of these studies was not to compare accounting frameworks. An accounting variable was added as a control for (the possible) accounting standard differences to trace the marginal effect of institutional factors. Results of the value relevance and informational asymmetries studies (Leuz, 2003; Bartov et al., 2002) should be supported by the accounting based earnings quality measures.

Another problem of research on the determinants of earnings management is the analysis of one determinant at a time. Studies try (mostly by research design) to trace an impact of a single earnings management determinant. However, it is more likely that a number of motivations drive accounting choice, which are then inhibited by a group of earnings management constraints. The similar notion can be found in Fields et al. (2001).

The following sections will try to close some of these gaps in the research on determinants of earnings management. The major purpose of the further sections is to provide empirical evidence on the impact of accounting standards and the competing determinants of earnings management on the extent of earnings quality.

4.4 Do Accounting Standards Influence the Level of Earnings Management? Evidence from Germany[52]

4.4.1 Hypothesis Development

The lack of a systematic analysis of accounting standards is partly due to the overall research design. Studies typically cover one single market to which only one set of standards applies. Cross-country analyses are difficult to interpret as institutional factors vary as do the standards themselves. Results will therefore very likely suffer from a severe omitted variable problem. Ideally, accounting standards are compared in a (approximately) constant institutional framework in which these accounting standards compete. Germany is such a case as listed companies may use German GAAP (HGB), IAS/IFRS and U.S. GAAP as alternative methods to report group earnings. Allowing alternative accounting treatments will possibly lead to alternative reporting practices and alternative levels of earnings management which depend on the design of the standards: Each set of standards may span a different and typical "topography" of the potential for earnings management. Actual reporting choices will allow to map this topography.

H_1^1: *Earnings of German companies that report under U.S. GAAP, IAS/IFRS or German GAAP do not have the same properties. The level of earnings management is not the same under all sets of standards.*

An observed difference in the extent of earnings management may be due to standards; it may also be explained by disclosure motivations. Firms may choose the standard that suits their disclosure interests most. Observed "standard effects" may therefore not reflect a regulatory (standard-driven) dimension, but may only reflect disclosure motivations.

The previous chapters have revealed the multi-faceted nature of motivations to manage earnings. When a multitude of long-term and short-term motivations drive reporting decisions in the overall economy, these partly commingling and contradictory motivations may create a "white noise" in which standard effects can be isolated. This does not mean that the choice of an accounting standard is random at the firm level – rational choice on this level is not denied. It means that the individual trade-offs do not add up to a coherent and measurable disclosure motivation.[53] In such a case, regulation and therefore standard setting has a genuine impact on an overall, economy-wide level.

[52] Parts of section 4.4 were used in the working paper "Do Accounting Standards Influence the Level of Earnings Management? Evidence from Germany" (Goncharov/Zimmermann, 2003).

[53] Epistemologically, this approach claims that commingling motivations create a veil of ignorance which can be modeled as randomness (e.g., Menges, 1968, p. 271). A competing approach would treat the phenomenon as an omitted variable problem (Fields et al., 2001, p. 291). With a lack of a coherent "disclosure theory" this latter approach is open to criticism such as ad-hoc model specifications.

To infer an isolated contribution of accounting standards the following hypothesis is tested:

H_1^2 *: Immediate disclosure motivations do not drive the choice of accounting standards on the firm level.*

If this hypothesis cannot be rejected, then this would provide some evidence that different accounting standards impact in specific ways on the extent to which earnings are managed.

4.4.2 Sample Review and Model Specification

4.4.2.1 Data and Sample Review

The sample includes German companies from DAX 30, MDAX and NEMAX 50[54] in the years 1996 to 2002. Companies listed in the above mentioned indexes are very appealing for the research purposes as they are using different accounting standards but are still operating in the German capital market. Germany has been witnessing a long phase of transition in corporate reporting. To improve their appeal to international investors, many German listed companies started to report consolidated earnings under international rather than domestic accounting rules. Para. 292a of the German Commercial Code (HGB) allows consolidated earnings to be reported using an accepted international framework or the original German rules. In practice, results are reported under U.S. GAAP, IAS/IFRS or German GAAP.

Banks and insurance companies are excluded from the initial sample because they have different financial reporting environment and accrual processes (Peasnell et al., 2000). Foreign (i.e. American and Swiss) firms are also exclude to keep institutional factors constant. According to these criteria from 150 companies[55] 124 companies[56] are included in the sample. The analysis requires firms to have at least one financial data time series according to one set of accounting standards of four years (three accrual observations[57]) during the observation period. This is a necessary condition for the calculation of the earnings management metric. Because of these reason another 9 firms are dropped. The final sample size is 115 companies. Notice that firms are

[54] Listing status as of the year 2000.

[55] 30 companies listed in DAX 30, 70 listed in MDAX and 50 listed in NEMAX 50.

[56] Some companies underwent the process of mergers and acquisitions during the evidence period. For instance *Friedrich Krupp AG* merged with *Thyssen AG* forming *ThyssenKrupp AG*. In such cases financial reports of merged companies are included into analysis as soon as they were available.

[57] Accruals are computed as the difference between the present year and the past. Four firm-years therefore result in three accrual observations. The firm may have a maximum of six accrual observations during our seven year observation period.

dropped, not firm-years. If a company has reported under German GAAP for three years and then four years under international accounting framework, all observations are used: seven firm-years are used to predict managed accruals as this is done for the industry and four years are used to compute the earnings management metric.

Some of the companies have changed the reporting framework in the middle of the observation period. For such companies there are two data strings: 1996 to 1999 according to German GAAP and 1999 to 2002 according to international reporting standards. The number of such firms is six. Such data strings are considered as if they stem from two different companies of the same industry. Therefore the tests will be performed with the sample size of 121 data points (or in other words 121 earnings management metric observations). Out of possible 726 accrual observations, 633 can be utilized as the level of disclosure in some cases does not permit the calculation of accruals.

The research covers only earnings management of annual net income. Earnings from interim reports have different dynamics and are subject to manipulations using quarterly instruments (Mendenhall/Nichols, 1988, p. 64-65; Salamon/Stober, 1994, p. 300-302).

Table 5: Classification of accrual observations according to SIC[58]

SIC code (first digit)	Code description	Accrual observations					
		HGB		IAS/IFRS		U.S. GAAP	
		N	%	N	%	N	%
1	Mining and Construction	9	3	11	7	0	0
2	Food and Kindred Products	42	14	31	20	18	10
3	Manufacturing	81	26	28	18	30	17
4	Transportation and Communication	14	5	16	11	14	8
5	Sales	42	14	19	13	15	9
6	Financial Institutions and Insurance[59]	92	30	32	21	31	18
7	Services	22	7	13	9	48	28
8	Services	6	2	2	1	17	10
Total		308	100	152	100	173	100

Table 5 classifies the obtained accrual observations for the estimation period in accordance with the industries to which the companies belong. The sample data does not display obvious industry biases in any form.[60]

Table 6 presents the descriptive statistics of the sample. It shows that German GAAP, IAS/IFRS and U.S. GAAP firm years differ from each other in size.[61] Companies in the U.S. GAAP samples are smaller than those from the HGB and especially IAS/IFRS samples. The U.S. GAAP sample has the highest standard deviation as it includes firm years of such giants as *DaimlerChrysler AG* and years of many Neuer Markt companies that came into existence only in the nineties. The implications for economic consequences will be addressed later.

Table 6: Descriptive statistics for HGB, IAS/IFRS and U.S. GAAP firms

Parameter	Firm years		
	HGB	IAS/IFRS	U.S. GAAP
Revenues			
...mean	7.338.397	7.871.708	8.113.421
...median	1.899.099	2.425.443	181.697
...standard deviation	13.721.044	14.483.270	26.782.487
Total assets			
...mean	7.651.148	8.869.072	9.485.956
...median	1.381.902	2.594.250	237.905
...standard deviation	18.833.402	18.390.752	31.800.107

Parameters are measured in thousands EUR.

Financial data for the calculation and prediction of the accruals is taken from the Hoppenstedt Bilanzdatenbank or directly from the firms' annual reports.

4.4.2.2 SPECIFICATION OF AN AUXILIARY MODEL

The research design relies on the separation of discretionary and non-discretionary earnings components. For this separation, it is proposed to use the cash flow Jones model (with the Dechow et al. (1995) adjustment for the change in receivables).

Accruals can be separated into non-discretionary and discretionary components, with discretionary components being influenced by earnings management decisions. Nor-

[58] SIC codes are obtained from the Amadeus Database.

[59] Includes two-digit SIC codes 65 (Real estate) and 67 (Holding and other investment offices).

[60] The Kolmogorov-Smirnov test showed no differences between population distributions between accounting regimes sub-samples at the 28%, 66% and 98% significance levels for the comparison of German GAAP – IAS/IFRS, German GAAP – U.S. GAAP and U.S. GAAP – IAS/IFRS sub-samples respectively.

[61] During the period many companies from the sample switched from reporting under HGB to reporting under international accounting standards. The data from "international" statements was used to calsulate statistics as soon as it was possible.

mal accruals are used to proxy for the non-discretionary figures. These normal accruals are the part of the accruals that can be explained by the firms' economic circumstances using the cash flow Jones model (i.e. the difference between accruals and residual).[62]

$$AA_{it} = \alpha_1 + \alpha_2(\Delta REV_{it} - \Delta REC_{it}) + \alpha_3 PPE_{it} + \alpha_4 CFO_{it} + \varepsilon_{it}, \qquad (57)$$

Gross property, plant and equipment, revenues and cash flow from operations in the model (57) are the main drivers of the accrual process.[63] Revenues drive accounts receivable, accounts payable and inventory, and therefore working capital accruals (Jones, 1991, p. 213). The original Jones model assumes that revenues are non-discretionary (i.e. there is no improper revenue recognition).[64] Dechow et al. (1995) imply that managers have more discretion over recognition of the part of revenues that derive from sales on credit than over the part of revenues that derive from cash sales. Therefore, revenues in the modified Jones model are adjusted to the change of sales on credit.[65] Gross property, plant and equipment drive depreciation and amortization expense. Cash flow from operations is added because of the evidence of strong negative correlation between accruals and cash flows (e.g., Dechow, 1994).

The expected sign of change in revenues less change in receivables (i.e. α_2) is difficult to predict because revenues are related to income-increasing accruals as well as to income-decreasing accruals. However the empirical research showed a general tendency of this coefficient to be positive. The expected sign of property, plant and equipment (i.e. α_3) is negative because PPE is positively correlated with depreciation and amortization expense, which represents income-decreasing parts of accruals. The expected sign on cash flow from operations is predicted to be negative.

The level of earnings management is compared using a smoothing ratio. Following Pincus/Rajgopal (2002), it is defined as the ratio of standard deviation of non-discretionary earnings to the standard deviation of earnings. Non-discretionary accruals are residuals from the cash flow Jones model.

When management reduces the volatility of earnings by the use of discretionary accruals, this will result in smaller values of the standard deviation of net income. There-

62 All variables in the model are scaled by lagged assets to reduce the problem of heteroscedastic disturbance, see Jones (1991, p. 212).

63 I.e. the process under which the balance sheet entries due to accrual instead of cash accounting are made.

64 This assumption fails in practice. SEC reports 515 enforcement actions of financial reporting and disclosure violations from which 126 resulted from improper revenue recognition (see SEC, 2003, p. 6). Comparably to SEC findings Nelson et al. (2003) classify 114 of 515 earnings-management approaches as resulting from revenue and other gains recognition practices.

65 Dechow et al. (1995) make such an adjustment only in the event period. However, here revenues are adjusted for credit sales in every year. The similar approach was used by e.g. Kothari et al. (2002) and Pincus/Rajgopal (2002).

fore, volatility of earnings before abnormal accruals in excess of the volatility of net income indicates earnings smoothing activities. The values of the smoothing ratio in this case will be significantly larger than one.

This indirect measure is applied because it suits the research design better than using absolute values of discretionary earnings or components thereof. Straightforward (direct) accrual partitioning models require the researcher to determine a period in which the occurrence of a certain event is hypothesised or observed. Such an event is difficult to establish in the analysed setting.[66] Accounting academic literature also argues that German firms engage in substantial income smoothing (e.g., Ball et al., 2003; Leuz et al., 2003). While this approach is limiting in the sense that it only picks up a subset of earnings management, namely earnings smoothing behaviour, it will suffice to reject the null hypothesis. It is therefore powerful enough from a methodological perspective. Obtained mean (median) smoothing ratios for the sub-samples will be compared using a t-test (Wilcoxon rank-sum test).

The following model specification will be used to calculate the smoothing ratio:

$$SR_i = {}^{\sigma_{NDE\,(i)}}\!\big/_{\sigma_{E\,(i)}}, \tag{58}$$

where:

SR	=	smoothing ratio,
σ_{NDE}	=	standard deviation of non-discretionary earnings (NDE),
σ_E	=	standard deviation of earnings, and

$$NDE_i = CFO_i + NDACC_i, \tag{59}$$

4.4.3 Evidence of Earnings Management

4.4.3.1 Analysing the Extent of Earnings Management under Different Accounting Standards

The analysis starts with the estimation of non-discretionary accruals using the cash flow Jones model. OLS regressions are fitted cross-sectionally over the whole observation period with the 8 one-digit SIC code groups.[67] *Table 7* shows the mean statistics

---

66 It was considered using the event of the economic downturn in 2000. Such a specification would have been problematic as not all German firms suffer uniformly from an economic downturn. Further to this, Basu (1997) provides evidence that firms may manage earnings anticipating downturns, casting further doubts on the possibility to use this methodology.

67 Normal practice is to use the second digit SIC codes (see e.g., DeFond/Jiambalvo, 1994). Because of the lack of data points, here only the first digit SIC codes are analysed.

for the obtained regression coefficients.[68] White-adjusted standard errors are used throughout the article to control for remaining heteroscedasticity (White, 1980).

The sign of change in revenues less change in receivables (i.e. α_2) is positive in 7 out of 8 groups. The mean and median (results are not tabulated for a median) estimates are positive as well. The sign of regression coefficient for property, plant and equipment (i.e. α_3) is negative in 7 out of 8 regressions and the mean and median estimates are negative as expected. The mean and median estimates of a coefficient on cash flow from operations (i.e. α_4) are negative; the sign is negative in all regressions. The R^2 is at 72 percent.

Table 8 shows descriptive statistics for parameters used to calculate the smoothing ratio.

Table 7: Cash flow Jones model estimates

		Expected sign	Mean estimate *(Coeff. mean adj. t-stat.)*
Intercept	α_1	?	0,085 *(1,62)*
ΔREV – ΔREC	α_2	+	0,076 *(2,77)*
PPE	α_3	-	-0,302 *(-0,82)*
CFO	α_4	-	-0,707 *(-8,37)*
Average sample size			79
Average R^2			0,72

Regressions are performed with the 8 one-digit SIC code groups. Dependent variable in regressions is accounting accruals (AA), measured as a change in non-cash current accruals less depreciation expense. Independent variables are PPE (gross property, plant and equipment), ΔREV – ΔREC (change in revenues less change in accounts receivable) and CFO (cash flow from operations, measured as operating income less accounting accruals. All variables are scaled by lagged total assets).

The results indicate that there are significant differences between the U.S. GAAP results on the one side and German GAAP and IAS/IFRS on the other. The median smoothing ratios of the German GAAP, IAS/IFRS, U.S. GAAP samples equal 6,73; 5,08 and 3,28 respectively, giving an indication that substantial earnings management has occurred. According to the pair-wise comparison of the means/medians, the U.S. GAAP smoothing ratio differs from German GAAP and IAS/IFRS on the 5% significance level. However, we find no significant difference between the means/medians of the German GAAP and IAS/IFRS sub-samples.

[68] One extreme observation was dropped in the first-digit SIC code group 3. The value of accounting accruals for this observation was 332,28.

Table 8: Descriptive statistics for parameters used in the calculation of the smoothing ratio

	Statistics				
	Mean	Stand. deviation	Q1	Median	Q3
Earnings	1,01	23,21	0,04	0,04	0,08
Cash flow from operations	1,73	38,96	0,13	0,13	0,23
Non-discretionary accruals	-0,61	16,46	0,01	0,01	0,13

Obtained parameters are further incorporated the in an earnings management metric, the smoothing ratio. *Panel B* of *Table 9* presents the comparison of the means and medians of the smoothing ratio for the three accounting regime sub-samples.

Table 9: Earnings management under different accounting regimes

Panel A: Smoothing ratio

	Mean	Median
German GAAP	11,38	6,73
IAS/IFRS	13,68	5,08
U.S. GAAP	5,57	3,28

Panel B: Differences in the levels of the smoothing ratio

	Two-sided p-values of a t-test	Two-sided p-values of a Wilcoxon-test
German GAAP – IAS/IFRS	0,59	0,99
German GAAP – U.S. GAAP	0,02	0,00
IAS/IFRS – U.S. GAAP	0,04	0,03

Earnings smoothing tests provide some evidence in respect to the hypothesis H_1^1 and show that there are substantial differences between earnings properties reported under different accounting standards, with U.S. GAAP data showing the lowest level of earnings smoothing. As there are no significant differences between the quality of German GAAP and IAS/IFRS earnings, additional tests will concentrate only on the differences between IAS/IFRS-German GAAP and U.S. GAAP firms.

4.4.3.2 Additional Tests

Following Leuz et al. (2003) two additional earnings management metrics are employed to identify performance differences between accounting standards. These additional tests help addressing the problem of the model estimation.

Leuz et al. (2003) suggest that low values of the ratio of the firm-level standard deviation of operating income to the standard deviation of cash flows σ(OpInc)/σ(CFO) may reveal information about the smoothing of earnings through accruals, i.e. about the level to which insiders reduce variability in reported income. The second measure is the correlation of changes in accruals and changes in cash flow from operations ρ(ΔAA;ΔCFO). Values of this measure close to –1 indicate smoothing of reported income that cannot be singly explained by the firm's economic performance.[69] The significance of the difference is determined with the t-test (Wilcoxon rank-sum test) and a test for differences in obtained values of correlation coefficients.[70] The results of the analysis are shown in the *Table 10.*

Table 10 shows that there are significant differences between the U.S. GAAP results on the one side and German GAAP-IAS/IFRS on the other. According to the pair-wise comparison of the means (medians), the U.S. GAAP mean (median) ratio of σ(OpInc)/σ(CFO) differs from German GAAP-IAS/IFRS on the 5% significance level. Results of the correlation analysis also indicate the higher quality of U.S. GAAP.

For German GAAP these results are widely supported on a theoretical level.[71] For IAS/IFRS the results may be explained by the purpose of IAS/IFRS. IAS/IFRS have to be flexible enough to be applied in different international circumstances. Thus IAS/IFRS may have to provide more opportunities to entities in different countries to treat events in the most appropriate way to their respective environments.

Hypothesis H_0^1 can be rejected: There are substantial differences between earnings properties reported under different accounting standards, with U.S. GAAP data showing the lowest level of earnings management.

69 Leuz et al. (2003) also use another two earnings management metrics. The median ratio of absolute accruals to absolute cash flows is used as a proxy for the overstatement of earnings to achieve certain thresholds. The forth metric (defined as the number of small profits divided by the number of small losses) proxies for loss avoidance. Both metrics is of little relevance for this research context as mainly the smoothing issues are addressed.

70 Computed as $Z = \dfrac{\left(0{,}5 * \ln\left(\dfrac{1+\rho_1}{1-\rho_1}\right) - 0{,}5 * \ln\left(\dfrac{1+\rho_2}{1-\rho_2}\right)\right)}{\sqrt{\dfrac{1}{n_1-3}+\dfrac{1}{n_2-3}}}$.

71 See e.g., Meitner et al. (2002, p. 140), Born (2001, p. 27), Müller/Wulf (2001, p. 2206).

4.4.4 Testing for Immediate Disclosure Motivations

A major obstacle for generalising the findings from the rejection of H_0^1 stems from a concern that these results may suffer from self-selection bias. The analysed firms choose accounting standards. For this reason, it may be the case that the distribution of accounting standards across them is not random. Firms with growth opportunities and financing needs may choose standards with perceived higher quality than firms with low financing needs. The latter firms may be also likely to engage in more earnings management. Thus, the rejection of H_0^1 could be driven entirely by self-selection and not the accounting standards themselves.

Table 10: Earnings management measures

	σ(OpInc)/σ(CFO)		ρ(ΔAA;ΔCFO)	
	Mean	Median	Pearson	Spearman
German GAAP-IAS/IFRS	0,46	0,30	-0,96	-0,90
U.S. GAAP	0,66	0,61	-0,62	-0,60
Difference[72]	-0,21**	-0,31**	-1,18***	-0,80***

*,**,*** - indicate significance on the 10%, 5% and 1% level respectively (two-tailed tests).

This possible bias is tested in the following way. As managers choose to apply a set of standards at a given point in time, it is analysed whether the outcomes of these choices are related to the disclosure motivations that can be identified for the firm. If a strong relationship is found between the choice of a reporting framework and the motivations for disclosure, it is likely that self-selection drives the results of the previous chapters. In such a case, it is not possible to isolate a constraining function of an accounting standard.

The testing procedures require to identify the year in which a company decided to report under an international accounting standard. In the sample some companies embraced an international framework during the observation period, and some continued to report under their original format. For the group of firms that began to report under either IAS/IFRS or U.S. GAAP in the observation period, the year of the accounting standard's choice is defined as one year before the first financial report under international framework was available. A small number of firms (from NEMAX 50) that came into existence after 1996 chose to report under IAS/IFRS or U.S. GAAP from the outset. For these firms the year prior to listing is the decision year. Four years were identified, in which decisions to report under the international framework took place. These are the years 1996 to 1999. The average year of first application of international frameworks (i.e. 1997) is used as the decision year for firms that decided to continue

[72] The difference for the correlation coefficients is normalized.

reporting under German GAAP. The univariate tests will be followed by a multivariate probit regression.

The literature typically identifies the following four drivers that capture influences on disclosure decisions: profitability, size, future financing needs and leverage.[73] These drivers will be used for the following analysis.

For the univariate test, first the numerical metrics are computed and then compared against reference groups. To assess a reporting decision, the obtained firm-specific metrics are compared against three reference groups: the group out of which the firm opts, the group into which the firm opts, and the whole sample.[74] All groups are constructed specifically for each decision year. This year-wise comparison mitigates against problems with inflation, exchange rate fluctuations and economic downturns.

The observations are then grouped according to high, middle and low performance. The 0,25 and 0,75 percentiles are calculated for this purpose. Then the number of firms is calculated in each of the sub-samples (German GAAP, IAS/IFRS and U.S. GAAP) with the observations below, within and above the 0,25 and 0,75 percentiles. The result of this procedure is a construction of a 3x3 contingency table. If the value of the χ^2-statistic for this table is below the critical value the conclusion is that the two attributes (accounting standard and the magnitude of the firm characteristic) are independent of each other. All calculations remained robust in respect to in-group, out-group and whole-sample computations. In the following, the tables will only report the results for the whole-sample comparison.

Table 11 shows the lower and upper boundaries of economic circumstances for the whole sample for the decision years 1996 to 1999.[75]

Table 11: Percentiles of the economic circumstances for the whole sample

Economic	Disclosure motivations							
circumstances	1996		1997		1998		1999	
	25%	75%	25%	75%	25%	75%	25%	75%
ROA	0,01	0,06	0,02	0,07	0,02	0,06	0,01	0,06
Firm size	11,71	15,17	11,18	15,26	11,75	15,27	12,35	15,39
Financing needs	0,05	0,32	0,06	0,32	0,03	0,37	0,03	0,28
Leverage	0,62	0,81	0,57	0,80	0,57	0,78	0,47	0,76

[73] See Leuz (2003) for further details.

[74] With the exception of the driver future financing needs where not enough data was available. Here, it is only possible to compare against the whole-sample and the out-group.

[75] Extremely high revenue growth (i.e. financing needs) is obviously related to acquisitions. As many acquisitions were financed by share issues, both organic and acquisitive growth is indicative of financing needs.

Panel A of *Table 12* shows the classification of firms according to its profitability level. Profitability is measured as return on assets at the end of each decision year. The choice of accounting regime is independent from the level of profitability on the 5% level.

Firm size is defined as the natural logarithm of total assets at the end of the decision year. The percentiles for the whole sample are shown in *Table 11.* The χ^2-test in the *Panel B* of *Table 12* shows no dependence between the attributes on the 5% level.

Table 12: Classification of firms' observations according to economic circumstances

Panel A: Classification of firms' observations according to ROA			
Accounting regime	Low	Middle	High
German GAAP	13	31	11
IAS/IFRS	4	16	9
U.S. GAAP	14	12	11
		N = 121 $\chi^2 = 0,83$	
Panel B: Classification of firms' observations according to firm size			
German GAAP	5	38	12
IAS/IFRS	10	10	9
U.S. GAAP	20	12	5
		N = 121 $\chi^2 = 3,65$	
Panel C: Classification of firms' observations according to future financing needs			
German GAAP	20	31	4
IAS/IFRS	5	13	11
U.S. GAAP	5	17	15
		N = 121 $\chi^2 = 2,80$	
Panel D: Classification of firms' observations according to leverage			
German GAAP	10	35	10
IAS/IFRS	7	12	10
U.S. GAAP	7	13	17
		N = 121 $\chi^2 = 1,50$	

The proxy for the need for future financing is the actual average rate of revenue growth per year from the year the company applied the new reporting standard until 2002. *Panel C* of *Table 12* shows the classification of firms according to the future financing needs. The χ^2-test showed that the two attributes are independent from each other on the 5% level.

The last firm characteristic that was tested is the leverage defined as the ratio of debt to the total assets at the end of the decision year. The percentiles of the leverage are shown in the *Table 11.* The choice of accounting standard is independent from the magnitude of leverage on the 5% level (*Panel D* of *Table 12*).

The univariate tests show no relation between immediate disclosure motivations and the choice of a reporting standard. As classifying firms into three bins obviously destroys information, it is necessary to support univariate results with additional multivariate tests.

The analysis in the previous section has shown no significant differences between IAS/IFRS and German GAAP. Therefore, the probit model in this section is estimated for differences in standard choice between IAS/IFRS-German GAAP and U.S. GAAP firms. On the left-hand side of the model is a binary variable taking values 0 for German GAAP-IAS/IFRS firms and 1 for U.S. GAAP firms. This binary variable is regressed on constant, return on assets, firm size, financing needs, leverage and 7 one-digit SIC code dummy variables (see model (60)). Following Leuz (2003) and the extant literature on discretionary disclosure, the choice of a higher quality accounting standard (i.e. U.S. GAAP) is a positive function of firm size and future financing needs. Firm-performance may be both positively and negatively associated with the discretionary disclosure according to the type of information provided (Leuz, 2003, p. 308). Botosan/Frost (1998) provide evidence that greater disclosure is provided by more highly leveraged (leverage is defined by the authors as a ratio of long-term debt to equity) U.S.-listed foreign companies. Industry dummies are included to control for competitors' standard choice (Leuz, 2003, p. 308).

$$AccSt_i = \alpha_1 + \alpha_2 ROA_i + \alpha_3 \ln(A_i) + \alpha_4 FN_i + \alpha_5 Lev_i + \sum_j \alpha_j Ind_{ji} + \varepsilon_i, \qquad (60)$$

where:

AccSt	=	dummy variable taking a value of one if company reports under U.S. GAAP and zero if a company reports either under German GAAP or IAS/IFRS,
FN	=	financing needs, measured as actual average rate of revenue growth per year from the year the company applied the new reporting standard until 2002,
Lev	=	leverage, measure as the ratio of debt to total assets, and
Ind_j	=	a set dummy variables representing first-digit SIC code industry groups.

Table 13 reports the results of the probit analysis. White-adjusted standard errors are used to control for misspecifications of the underlying distribution (White, 1982). The signs on financing needs and leverage are as predicted positive but not significant. The firm size is significant at the 5% level, but has an unexpected sign. The pseudo R^2 is low. This is consistent with the "white noise" hypothesis in which standard effects can be isolated: It means that the individual trade-offs do not add up to a coherent and measurable disclosure motivation so that the constraints in the standards appear as overall binding.

Table 13: Standard choice analysis

		Expected sign	Model estimated coefficients *(White-adj. z-statistic/p-value)*
Intercept	α_1	?	1,039 *(0,97/0,33)*
ROA	α_2	?	-0,220 *(-1,25/0,21)*
LnA	α_3	+	-0,137 *(-2,33/0,02)*
FN	α_4	+	0,001 *(0,26/0,79)*
Lev	α_5	+	0,605 *(1,11/0,27)*
Ind_j	α_j	?	Included
Sample size			121
Pseudo R^2			0,16

Results of the probit analysis. Dependent variable: AccSt – a dummy variable taking a value of one if company reports under U.S. GAAP and zero if a company reports either under German GAAP or IAS/IFRS. Independent variables: FN – financing needs (measured as actual average rate of revenue growth per year from the year the company applied the new reporting standard until 2002), Lev – leverage (measure as the ratio of debt to total assets), ROA – return on assets, Indj - a set dummy variables representing first-digit SIC code industry groups. Standard errors are adjusted to control for misspecifications of the underlying distribution.

In summary, no evidence is found that the choice of an accounting standard is dependent on immediate disclosure motivations. However, these results must be taken with some caution. Unlike the previous hypothesis, H_0^2 could not be rejected. Effects may simply not have been captured in the used variables, or the testing procedures may not have been powerful enough. The robustness of the results though encourages to draw some additional conclusions on the quality of accounting standards themselves.

4.4.5 Concluding Remarks for the Role of Accounting Standards

The analysis showed that earnings management is widely spread in Germany but that there are differences when the reporting framework is considered. Firms that report under U.S. GAAP engage in earnings management practices less often than firms that report under German GAAP or IAS/IFRS. Between those two frameworks, the level of earnings management is broadly the same. These results hold for the tests using the concept of discretionary accruals (i.e. the smoothing ratio) and for the additional tests of earnings smoothing.

Further testing showed that accounting standards have a different effectiveness in constraining earnings management: Tests show no significant relationship between those economic factors that motivate disclosure decisions, earnings management and the choice of a reporting framework. A lower level of earnings management in U.S. GAAP therefore indicates that U.S. GAAP mitigates more effectively against earnings management than German GAAP or IAS/IFRS. As these conclusions are reached by joint hypotheses on disclosure motivations and observable levels of earnings management, this finding may depend on the methodology and is open to further query.

4.5 REPORTING BEHAVIOUR WHEN INCENTIVES COMPETE: THE ROLE OF TAX ACCOUNTING IN RUSSIA[76]

4.5.1 TAX MANAGEMENT OF RUSSIAN PRIVATE AND PUBLIC FIRMS

Tax management is defined as a reduction of the present value of income tax expense. While empirical research has documented a general tendency of companies in developed economies to manage taxes (e.g. Kasanen et al., 1996; Cushing/LeClere, 1992; Keating/Zimmerman, 2000; Scholes et al., 1992; Maydew, 1997; Gramlich, 1991), the tax management behaviour in transition economies has not yet been systematically addressed. The Russian economy seems a particularly rewarding case as priors such as institutional and cultural features in Russia point to a great extent of tax management: Only 16% of the companies paid their tax obligations fully and on time in the end of 1990s (Ledeneva/Kurkchiyan, 2000, p. 129). A poll showed that merely 29% of businessmen found tax evasion wrong (Klyamkin/Timofeev, 2000). When tax considerations are an important driver of financial reporting decisions, companies are likely to manage financial earnings downwards either through different accounting choices or through cash flow decisions, inter alia through removing certain cash flows from the balance sheets (i.e. fraud accounting).[77] The following hypothesis is formulated:

H_1^1 : *Russian companies manage earnings downwards to reduce (the present value of) taxes. Achievable economic benefits drive the extent of tax management.*

Tax management – be it by accrual choices or by incomplete reporting – lowers the quality of reported accounting earnings, which the market uses for assessing economic performance. Private and public firms are affected by the market pressure for high-quality accounting earnings to a different extent. Market forces create incentives to

[76] Parts of section 4.5 were used in the working paper "Earnings Management when Incentives Compete: The Role of Tax Accounting in Russia" (Goncharov/Zimmermann, 2004).

[77] An estimated 20% of the import sales in 2001 belonged to the "white" or official economy, 10% were criminal and the rest was "half legal" or so called "grey economy". That means that most of the firms operate in such a way that they show only a part of their business to the tax authorities (Radaev, 2002, p. 70).

report high quality accounting numbers. These incentives may vary significantly across firms (depending on e.g., legal form, listing status). This analysis concentrates on private and public firms. Owners of public firms must rely on publicly available data to effectively evaluate and monitor a company's performance. Investors prefer to trade in shares of firms reporting accounting data of high quality that is suitable for valuation and/or monitoring. By demanding a higher cost of capital from firms with low quality earnings, investors push firms to supply accounting information of a higher quality (e.g., Burgstahler et al., 2004). Firms without a listing status usually have a concentrated ownership and communicate information via private channels. In this case a firm's performance is assessed through private communication rather than through the analysis of accounting information. Recent empirical evidence supports this argument (e.g. Ball/Shivakumar, forthcoming, Burgstahler et al., 2004). These leads to the following hypothesis:[78]

H_1^2 : *Russian private companies manage taxes to a greater extent than Russian public companies.*

Russia's economic reforms established a company tax system in December 1991. The laws that regulated income taxes were the Law of 27.12.1991, N 2116-1, *On Income Taxes of Enterprises and Organizations* and the Regulation of 05.08.1992, N 552, *On Production Cost Allocation and Conditions of Financial Results Calculation.* The same laws with adjustments and amendments regulated the taxation of legal entities in 2001. According to the Law of 27.12.1991 certain expenses were not tax deductible and additional expenses could be claimed for deduction (see *Table 14* for examples of such expenses). Except for a different treatment of service lives for depreciable property and bad debt there were no differences between the tax and financial accounting. Tax and financial accounting were aligned to a very high level until 2002.

With the introduction of Chapter 25 of the Second Part of the *Tax Code* in 2002 that regulated income taxes the situation changed dramatically (see *Table 14*). The law makers tried to separate the two systems of financial and tax accounting (Bakaev, 2002, p. 95). Companies had to develop two accounting policies: one for book and one for tax accounting. The accounting policy for tax purposes included the following options: a choice of service lives of depreciable assets (par. 258) and depreciation methods (par. 259), method for recording uncollectibles (par. 266), the maximum amount of guarantee reserve (par. 267), the method for allocation of interest on debt (par. 269),

[78] Apart from the demand for accounting information there is also another reason for the difference in the extent of the tax management between private and public firms. Public companies face higher financial reporting costs, i.e. opportunity costs related to reporting lower income numbers in financial statements (e.g., Cloyd et al., 1996; Mills/Newberry, 2001). These costs are related to debt covenant constraints and breaking of earnings patterns. Public companies are less likely to take confirming positions in financial and tax accounting to manage earnings downwards and to reduce the present value of taxes (Mikhail, 1999).

revenue recognition and matching of expenses by accrual basis for tax purposes (par. 271).

Table 14: Changes in the income tax regulation

	2001	2002
Tax regulation	- Law of 27.12.1991, *On Income Taxes*; - Regulation of 05.08.1992, *On Production Cost Allocation*	- Chapter 25 of the Second Part of the Tax Code
Object of taxation	gross profit (practically: corrected EBT from the Income statement)	output from the tax accounting system
Policy choices for tax purposes	none	- service lives and depreciation methods for assets; - method for recording uncollect-ibles; - the maximum amount of guaran-tee reserves; - method for allocation of interest etc.
Tax relieves	- CAPEX in excess of depreciation; - R&D costs (<10% of EBT); - expenses for social items etc.	none
Expenses that cannot be (can be partly) reimbursed	- advertising costs in excess of certain percent of revenues; - interest costs in excess of certain amount etc.	practically none
Top statutory tax rate	35%	24%

The change in the Law on Income taxes that took place during 2001 provided an opportunity for firms to separate their financial and tax accounting systems in 2002. The purpose of tax accounting would be then accounting for taxes and minimization of current tax expenditures. The financial accounting system could be used to report high quality accounting numbers to provide investors and other stakeholders with information about the real economic performance of the company. Therefore, the new tax regulation provided an option to change the quality of reported earnings. This option, however, is likely to be exercised differently by private and public firms. Public firms that face a higher demand for their accounting data are more likely to separate financial and tax accounting to report earnings of superior information content. For private firms, the situation is likely to remain unchanged: For them, tax authorities are practically the only users of accounting information (Gorbatova, 2000, p. 105)[79], and there is a view that the major role of financial accounting is calculation of the tax expense (Preobragenskaya/McGee, 2004, p. 32). Beyond that, the setup of a complementary financial accounting system is costly (Bakaev, 2002, p. 60) and therefore economically attractive only for bigger firms.

It is predicted that the change in the Law on Income Taxes in 2002 had a differential effect on public and private firms:

H_1^3 : *The extent of the tax management of Russian private companies changed to a different degree than the extent of tax management of public companies after a change in reporting environment.*

The year 2000 also witnessed a major change in tax enforcement. The Tax Police have received more resources and power to decrease the number of tax avoidance schemes and to bring their users to court. Leuz et al. (2003) and Lang et al. (2004) show that enforcement affects the extent of earnings management.The legal enforcement on tax affected public and private companies in a different way. Tax enforcement and criminal charges were mostly oriented against big public companies. Desai et al. (2003) provide several examples of the tax-enforcement related cases against listed companies. These cases had a signalling role: The government showed that "...the tax avoidance behaviour will no longer be tolerated..." (Desai et al., 2003, p. 16). Relatively small private companies did not experience any considerable influence of this trend. These effects may also impact on the amount of change in tax management practices as the extent of fraud accounting is reduced.

4.5.2 Data and Sample Review

The sample consists of Russian companies from Bureau van Dijk's Amadeus and Osiris data banks. The observation periods are the years 2001 and 2002. Lagged values of variables from the year 2000 are used for scaling. These years are very appealing for research purposes because of several reasons. First the new Chapter of the Tax Code brought major changes into accounting for income taxes from the beginning of 2002. Second the inflation during the period 2000 to 2002 was relatively low and remained stable (annual average consumer price inflation was 20,8%; 21,6% and 15,1% in years 2000 to 2002 respectively).

The initial sample from the Amadeus data bank contained 22.042 private and 175 public companies. As much as 45 public companies were obtained from the Osiris data

79 A poll showed that 93% of accountants identified Tax service as the main user of accounting information (Rozhnova, 2000).

bank. Testing procedures require to delete firm-year observations of those companies that did not have all necessary financial information during the whole observation period. To keep the set of motivations for earnings management as homogeneous as possible, the state owned companies were excluded from the sub-group of private firms. Financial companies were also excluded from the initial sample (where such identification was possible), i.e. primary SIC codes 6011-6799, because they have a dissimilar reporting environment (e.g., banks are additionally controlled by the Central Bank of Russian Federation) and their accrual process is different. Double entries of public companies that were present on both Amadeus and Osiris data banks are not included into the samples. As a result from the possible 22.042 private and 220 public companies it was possible to obtaine 805 private and 39 public firm observations in the years 2001 and 2002. Only earnings numbers derived from the annual reports are within the scope of analysis.[80]

Data banks provided no information on industry codes of 385 private and 3 public firms (or about 46% of the whole sample). This makes it impossible to test any industry-related implications.

Table 15 classifies the obtained observations according to the legal form. Most of the companies in the sample are open-stock companies (47,8%), followed by the closed-stock companies (38,2%). The minor part of the sample (about 6%) represents other legal forms.

Table 15: Classification of observations according to the legal form

Abbreviation	Legal form description	Observations	
		N	%
OAO Private	Open joint-stock company (unlisted)	365	43,2
OAO Public	Open joint-stock company (listed)	39	4,6
ZAO	Closed joint-stock society	308	36,5
OOO	Limited liability society	85	10,1
Other		47	5,6
Total		844	100,0

Table 16 presents the descriptive statistic of the sample separately for the years 2001 and 2002. The mean revenues of private firms increased by 31,8% during the year 2002 while staying almost on the same level for public firms. The standard deviation of revenues grew by 52,9% for private firms and decreased by 17,3% for public firms,

80 No interim reports were available.

indicating differences in the growth rates of the companies. Mean total assets change was 18,8% and 20,5% for private and public firms respectively.

4.5.3 Evidence of Tax Management

Earnings management is defined broader than that currently used in other studies as the shadow economy in the Russian Federation is considered to be relatively large (e.g., Shleifer/Treisman, 2000; Yakovlev, 1998). Thus Russian companies may use additional forms of earnings management. Traditional concepts of earnings management comprise managers' judgments in financial reporting and structuring of business transactions to mislead some stakeholders of the company (e.g., Healy/Wahlen, 1999). Beyond using judgements in financial reporting or structuring transactions and timing of decisions affecting cash flows companies may also discretionary decide which fraction of their business operations they want to show on the balance sheets.

Table 16: Descriptive statistic for private and public firms

Parameter	Firm years			
	2001		2002	
	Private	Public	Private	Public
Revenues				
...mean	465.697	89.226.232	613.913	89.130.477
...median	136.511	4.220.745	164.903	14.387.962
...standard deviation	1.291.196	279.118.719	1.974.093	230.878.457
Total assets				
...mean	481.256	122.505.237	571.616	147.577.756
...median	97.834	9.827.380	117.422	19.559.173
...standard deviation	1.962.421	382.053.294	2.395.990	412.119.432

Parameters are measured in thousands RUB (denominated roubles).

Distributional tests as in Burgstahler/Dichev (1997) are implemented to consider the impact of motivations on earnings management behaviour of Russian companies. The idea beyond the tests is that the number of observations of scaled earnings (levels or changes) will be underrepresented in "unfavourable" intervals of the distribution and overrepresented in "favourable" intervals. For example, listed companies facing capital market pressure avoid reporting small losses and small earnings decreases. The number of observations in the interval just below zero will be then underrepresented and just above zero overrepresented for both earnings levels and changes plots, consistent with the developed hypotheses.

Distributional tests are the most suitable instrument to study earnings management in the current research design. These tests can trace earnings management via accruals and operating cash flows (Burgstahler/Dichev, 1997). The argument here is that this kind of analysis may also detect fraud accounting when an appropriate scale measure is used. Consider a situation in which a company is engaged in fraud accounting. To reduce taxes the company may remove some revenue flows from the income statement. In this case earnings will be smaller. The extent to which this removal can be permanent is questionable. However it is likely that if a company "hides" some revenues in one year it will also opt to "hide" them in the next year (especially in the case when a company removes revenue flows from the whole business line). Scaling earnings by lagged revenues will make fraud undetectable. Companies are not expected to remove assets (and especially fixed assets) from the balance sheets. First assets are expensed and reduce the tax base. Second it is often hard to "hide" assets. Thus scaling earnings by lagged assets will make fraud accounting visible. A possible detection of fraud accounting by distributional tests is a very attractive feature for the research design as private firms are expected to be more engaged in fraud accounting than earnings management via accrual or cash flow decisions.

Two important features of the empirical implementation of the distributional tests are the choice of the bin width and the test statistic for testing the significance of an expected discontinuity. The optimal bin width is a positive function of the variability of data (i.e. interquartile range) and a negative function of the number of observations (e.g., Scott, 1992):[81]

$$h = 2(IQR)N^{-1/3}, \tag{61}$$

where:

h	=	optimal bin width,
IQR	=	interquartile range, and
N	=	number of observations.

For analysed sample optimal interval width equals 0,025.

Empirical tests rely on the statistic proposed by Burgstahler/Dichev (1997) with the expected number of observations equal to an average of the number of observations in the two adjacent intervals:

$$z = \frac{n_a - n_e}{\sigma}, \tag{62}$$

where:

[81] In respect to earnings management this formula for the bin width was implemented by e.g. Degeorge et al. (1999) and Coppens/Peek (2004).

z	=	test statistic approximately distributed under a Normal distribution,
n_a	=	actual number of observations in the interval,
n_e	=	expected number of observations in the interval, and
σ	=	standard deviation of the difference, calculated as:

$$\sigma = \sqrt{Np_j(1-p_j) + 0{,}25N(p_{j-1} + p_{j+1})(1 - p_{j-1} - p_{j+1})}\,, \tag{63}$$

where:

p_j	=	fraction of observations in the j-th interval.

Test results for the peak of the distribution are not reported as the significance of the difference tends to be overstated. To obtain firm specific estimates of earnings levels and to reduce heteroskedasticity problems in the multivariate analyses all observations are scaled by lagged total assets.

The analysis starts with the plot of distribution of earnings levels for the whole set of companies over the years 2001 and 2002. Coppens/Peek (2004) show the distribution of earnings levels for high versus low alignment European countries. The peak of the distribution in countries with high financial-tax alignment is the first positive interval and there is a discontinuity of the earnings levels distribution immediately to the right of the peak. The distribution of earnings levels in low alignment countries tends to be smooth to the right of zero. The explanation for that is straightforward. The companies are using the same accounting treatments for financial and tax accounts either because the tax and accounting rules are identical or because financial (tax) accounting rules are used for tax (financial accounting) purposes.[82] The *naïve* expectation for managed earnings levels would be that earnings are negative. In this case the companies would not have to pay taxes. However other reporting incentives may force companies to show small profits. For instance banks and trade creditors tend to be reference dependent and require positive earnings figures. Even if we consider tax planning as the unique driver of earnings management, there are still incentives to report small profits. Small losses in Russia increase political costs. Firms that report losses have an option to liquidate the firm if they do not await a recovery (Hayn, 1995). Therefore firms that report losses (and especially small losses) and do not close their operations may be considered as a target group for the next inquiry by the tax authorities. If earnings are managed for the tax purposes it is expected to find a concentrated number of observations in the first positive interval and a discontinuity immediately after this first interval.[83] The distribution of earnings levels in 2001-2002 is shown in *Figure 6*.[84]

Figure 6: Distribution of earnings levels in 2001-2002

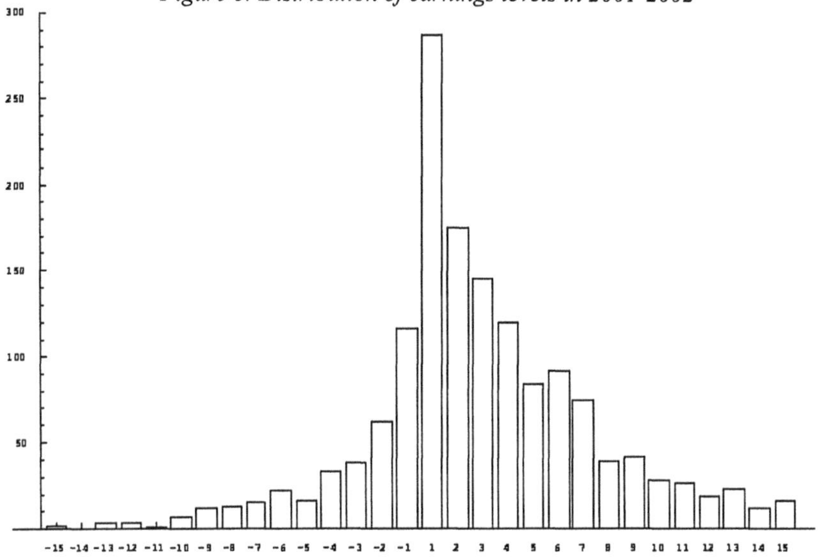

N = 1.688; h = 0,025

Distribution of earnings scaled by lagged total assets. The interval count is started at zero. Histogram is truncated to the 15-th interval on both sides of zero.

The histogram displays all attributes of an earnings distribution from a high financial and tax alignment country. The peak of the distribution coincides with the first interval and the number of observations in the second interval right of zero is underrepresented (z_{+2} = -2,69[85]; p = 0,01). Such behaviour may however result from several earnings management motivations, e.g. loss avoidance.

To shed more light on the influence of income taxes on the earnings management behaviour of Russian companies the whole sample is split into sub-samples of companies with high versus low motivations for tax-motivated earnings management. The magnitude of marginal tax rate discriminates between high and low incentives for earnings management (Keating/Zimmerman, 2000, p. 373). Contrasting these sub-samples will

---

[82] These three situations are referred to as "identity", "accounting leads" and "tax dominates" by Lamb et al. (1998).

[83] The earnings changes distribution is not considered. First it is not clear how earnings smoothing may effect tax management (Burgstahler et al., 2004). Second the effect of changing law environment on firm's decisions to smooth earnings cannot be predicted.

[84] The count of intervals starts from zero. For example the first positive interval (i.e. +1) is [0;0,025) and the first negative interval (i.e. -1) is [-0,025;0). Histograms are truncated to the 15-th interval on both sides of zero.

[85] The subscript of the test statistic shows the interval number.

provide some evidence whether earnings are managed downwards with the main motivation to reduce tax expenditure. The sample is split in each year into sub-samples conditional on the marginal tax rate, which is defined as taxes due for the period (or equally tax expense from income statement) divided by earnings before taxes. High incentive firms are those that have a marginal tax rate of more or equal to a top statutory tax rate (i.e. 35% in 2001 and 24% in 2002). Firms can pay income taxes in excess of the statutory tax rate when they have either no tax relieves or have expenditures that cannot be reimbursed.

Figure 7: Distribution of earnings levels for firms with low marginal tax rate in 2001 and 2002

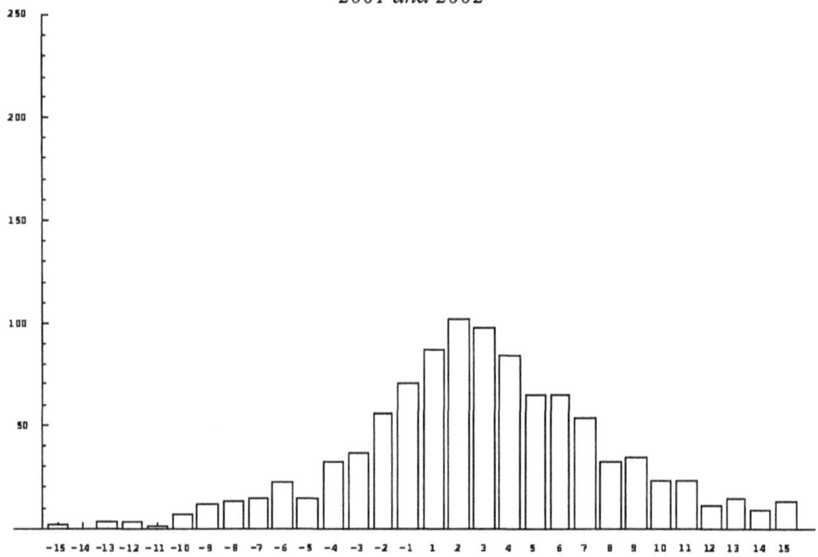

N = 1146; h = 0,025

Distribution of earnings scaled by lagged total assets. The interval count is started at zero. Histogram is truncated to the 15-th interval on both sides of zero.

If no tax management exists in the sub-sample of companies with a low marginal tax rate a distribution of earnings levels will be similar as for firms from the low alignment countries, i.e. a smooth distribution. The distribution of earnings levels for firms from the high marginal tax rate sub-sample will show a discontinuity between the first and second interval to the right of zero. *Figure 7* and *Figure 8* show the distribution of earnings levels in 2001 and 2002 for firms with low and firms with high marginal tax rate respectively.[86]

Figure 8: Distribution of earnings levels for firms with high marginal tax rate in 2001 and 2002

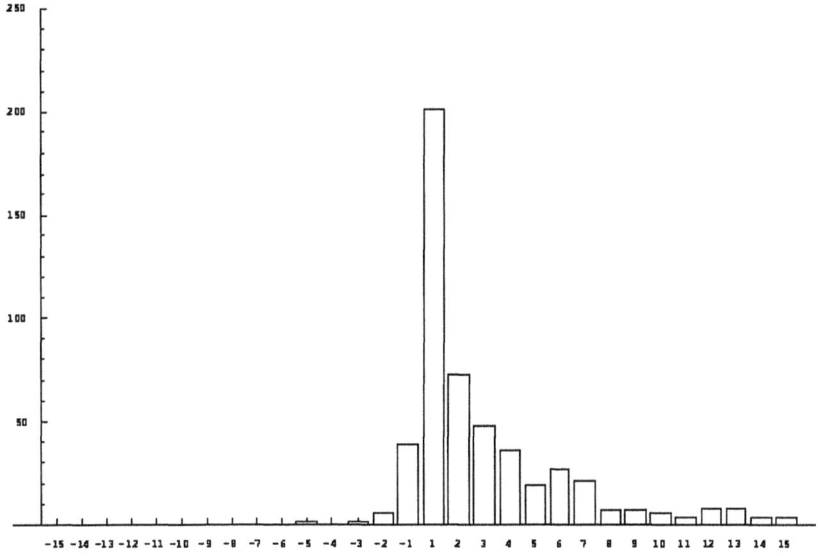

N = 537; h = 0,025

Distribution of earnings scaled by lagged total assets. The interval count is started at zero. Histogram is truncated to the 15-th interval on both sides of zero.

As expected the distribution in *Figure 7* is smoothly distributed to the right of zero. The peak of the distribution is the second positive interval. There are no discontinuities to the right of zero (z_{+1} = 0,05, p = 0,96; second interval z_{+2} = 0,87, p = 0,38; z_{+3} = 0,35, p = 0,72). A completely different situation is shown in the histogram of *Figure 8*. Here the peak of distribution coincides with the first positive interval. The number of observations in the second interval to the right of zero is statistically significant under-represented (z_{+2} = -5,24; p = 0,00). Contrasting the distributions of conditional sub-samples provides evidence consistent with the first hypothesis.

The following multivariate test is used to complement the univariate results. Phillips et al. (2003) propose to use a probit regression to investigate the importance of deferred tax expense for prediction of earnings management activities. The dependent variable

86 Five observations of private companies that had either zero earnings or both earnings and taxes equal zero were dropped.

in the regression model is an indicator variable taking the values of zero and one for the earnings observations lying in the bins of interest (i.e. zero, if the scaled earnings observation belongs to the first negative interval and unity, if the observation is from the first positive interval). On the right hand side they control for accruals and cash flow from operations as the vehicles for earnings management. The Amadeus and Osiris data banks do not provide information on depreciation and amortization expense for the Russian companies. Therefore, changes in working capital and a proxy for cash flow from operations as defined below are used instead of accruals and CFO.

The proxy variable is then added to assess the influence of taxation on earnings management. More specifically the sample partitioning criteria is used again as a dummy variable to proxy for the tax management. MTR takes the value of 1 for firms with a marginal tax rate over or equal to the top statutory tax rate and 0 otherwise. The following multivariate model is going to complement results of univariate tests:

$$EM_{it} = \alpha_0 + \alpha_1 \Delta WC_{it} + \alpha_2 CFOP_{it} + \alpha_3 MTR_{it} + \varepsilon_{it}, \qquad (64)$$

where:

EM	=	earnings management indicator variable, taking the value of 1 if the firm's earnings observation is in the first positive interval and 0 for all other intervals to the right of zero,
CFOP	=	cash flow from operations computed as operating income less changes in working capital, and
MTR	=	marginal tax rate, a binary variable equalling 1 if the firm's marginal tax rate is equal or higher than the top statutory tax rate and 0 otherwise.

The sign of coefficients on ΔWC and CFOP are predicted to be negative. The sign on MTR is predicted to be positive (i.e. the probability of reporting small earnings increases with the marginal tax rate).

Table 17 shows results of the regression analyses which addresses the effects of taxation on earnings management. White-adjusted standard errors are used to control for misspecifications of the underlying distribution (White, 1982). The sign on the control variables is as expected negative consistent with earnings management activities. The sign on MTR is positive and significant on the 1% level.

Results of the multivariate test confirm the univariate results for the first hypothesis: tax concerns were an important driver of earnings management of Russian companies.

4.5.4 INFLUENCE OF REPORTING INCENTIVES ON TAX MANAGEMENT

Only multivariate analysis is used to test the second hypothesis. One could consider comparing earnings distributions for the sub-sample of private and public firms. However the sample of public firms is too small to plot histograms and perform univariate statistical testing.

Table 17: Regression results for the effects of taxation

		Expected sign	Model estimated coefficients *(z-statistic/p-value)*
Intercept	α_0	?	-0,363 *(-2,60/0,01)*
ΔWC	α_1	-	-8,096 *(-5,87/0,00)*
CFOP	α_2	-	-8,031 *(-5,69/0,00)*
MTR	α_3	+	1,101 *(11,70/0,00)*
Sample size			1327
Pseudo R^2			0,36
Wald χ^2 *(p-value)*			152,99 *(0,00)*

Results of the probit analysis. Dependent variable: EM is earnings management indicator variable, taking the value of 1 if the firm's earnings observation is in the first positive interval and 0 for all other intervals to the right of zero. Independent variables: ΔWC is changes in working capital computed as changes in current assets less changes in cash minus changes in current liabilities less changes in shot-term debt (scaled by lagged total assets); CFOP is cash flow from operations computed as operating income less changes in working capital (scaled by lagged total assets) and MTR is marginal tax rate, a binary variable equalling 1 if the firm's marginal tax rate is equal or higher than the top statutory tax rate and 0 otherwise. Standard errors are adjusted to control for misspecifications of the underlying distribution.

The analysis inquires into the difference in the level of tax management between private and public firms by adding a dummy variable and an interaction term into the probit model. More specifically a PUBLIC dummy variable is added that takes values of one for public firms and zero for private firms. No predictions are made about the sign on PUBLIC. An interaction term of PUBLIC and MTR is added then into the model (64). The sign on the interaction variable is predicted to be negative consistent with tax management as a less important financial reporting attribute of public companies. *Table 18* provides the results of the probit regression.

The coefficient on MTR remains highly significant. The coefficient on the interaction variable is negative and significant on the 5% level. A negative and significant coefficient on the marginal MTR*PUBLIC is consistent with H_1^2.

Table 18: Regression results for differences in tax management levels between private and public firms

		Expected sign	Model estimated coefficients *(z-statistic/p-value)*
Intercept	α_0	?	-0,390 *(-2,77/0,01)*
ΔWC	α_1	-	-8,124 *(-5,88/0,00)*
CFOP	α_2	-	-8,058 *(-5,70/0,00)*
MTR	α_3	+	1,152 *(11,72/0,00)*
PUBLIC	α_4	?	0,450 *(1,78/0,07)*
MTR*PUBLIC	α_5	-	-0,817 *(2,33/0,02)*
Sample size			1327
Pseudo R^2			0,37
Wald χ^2 *(p-value)*			153,65 *(0,00)*

Results of the probit analysis. Dependent variable: EM is earnings management indicator variable, taking the value of 1 if the firm's earnings observation is in the first positive interval and 0 for all other intervals to the right of zero. Independent variables: ΔWC is changes in working capital computed as changes in current assets less changes in cash minus changes in current liabilities less changes in shot-term debt (scaled by lagged total assets); CFOP is cash flow from operations computed as operating income less changes in working capital (scaled by lagged total assets); MTR is marginal tax rate, a binary variable equalling 1 if the firm's marginal tax rate is equal or higher than the top statutory tax rate and 0 otherwise and PUBLIC is a public dummy, a binary variable equalling 1 for public firms and 0 for private firms. Standard errors are adjusted to control for misspecifications of the underlying distribution.

To test the third hypothesis, univariate tests are first performed for the sub-sample of private firms. No differences are expected in tax management of private firms between 2001 and 2002. As discussed above the distribution of earnings levels in high versus low financial-tax alignment countries look different. If the change in reporting environment between 2001 and 2002 changed also the extent of earnings management we will see an alteration in the distribution. According to this scenario the distribution for the high incentives sub-sample in 2001 would be peaked with a discontinuity between the first and second interval to the right of zero. In 2002 the distribution will tend to be smooth. *Figure 9* and *Figure 10* show the distribution of earnings levels for private firms with high marginal tax expense in 2001 and 2002 respectively.

The peak of distribution in 2001 is in the first interval and the number of observations in the second positive interval is statistically significantly underrepresented (z_{+2} = -3,27; p = 0,00). The histogram in 2002 has also all attributes of the earnings distribution from a high financial and tax alignment country. The peak coincides with the first interval and the number of observations in the second interval right of zero is under-represented (z_{+2} = -3,60; p = 0,00).

Figure 9: Distribution of earnings levels for private firms with high marginal tax rate in 2001

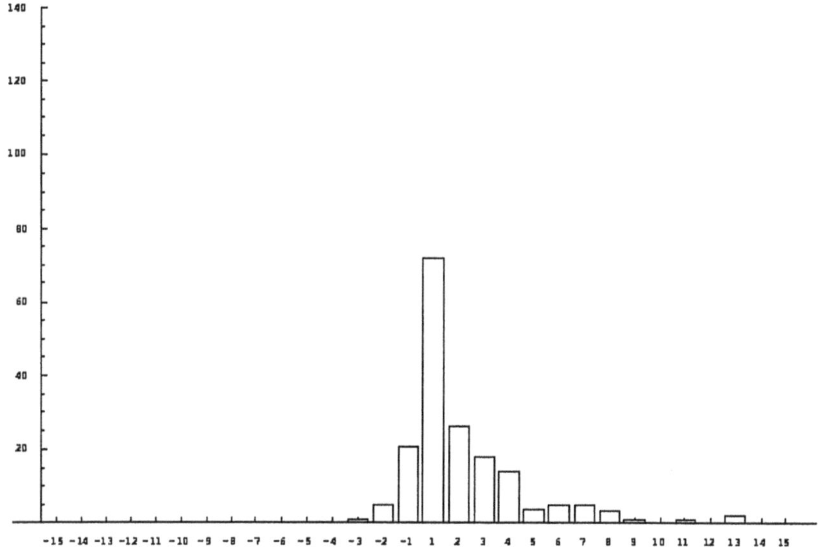

N = 184; h = 0,025

Distribution of earnings scaled by lagged total assets. The interval count is started at zero. Histogram is truncated to the 15-th interval on both sides of zero.

Surprisingly, tax management seems to be even more prevalent for private firms in 2002. There is the following explanation for this. Changing tax laws gave birth to uncertainties about tax expenses in 2002 as most of tax relieves were abandoned and the new tax system was not fully understood by accountants, which in turn may have caused the companies to pay penalties for wrong/not in-time paying of taxes (Bakaev, 2002, p. 60). Therefore the firms may have even stronger tax management incentives in 2002. Furthermore, companies could use the financial accounting system to calculate the income taxes due (Bakaev, 2002, p. 61). This means that although on the regulative level the financial and tax alignment ceased to exist, the incentives for following the tax rules in financial reporting became even stronger in 2002 (recall that all relieves and a number of not reimbursed expenditures were cancelled). This argument is tested by comparing the tax and financial earnings alignment in 2001 and 2002.

Figure 10: Distribution of earnings levels for private firms with high marginal tax rate in 2002

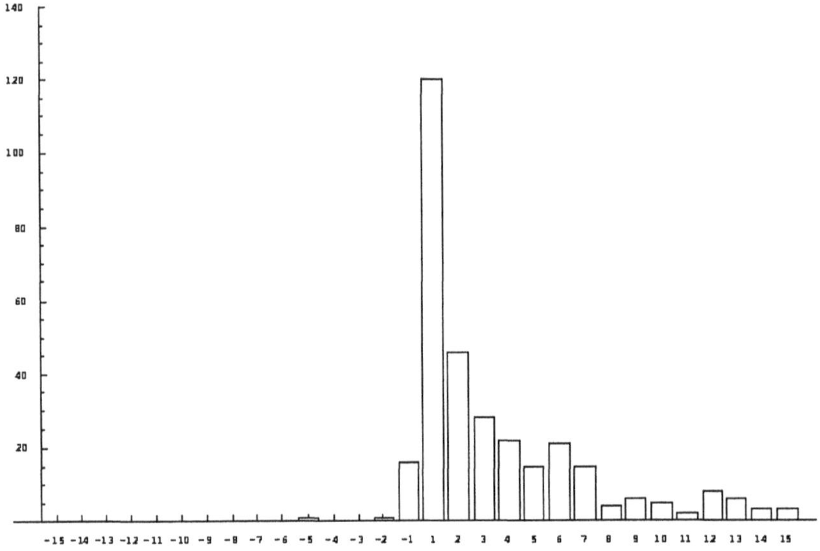

N = 337; h = 0,025

Distribution of earnings scaled by lagged total assets. The interval count is started at zero. Histogram is truncated to the 15-th interval on both sides of zero.

The financial and tax alignment is defined as the absolute difference between tax expense from the Income statement divided by the top statutory tax rate (i.e. 35% in 2001 and 24% in 2002) and earnings before taxes, scaled by the lagged total assets. The cases with the taxes paid equalling zero were excluded from the analysis. The median financial and tax alignment of private firms in 2002 is 0,038. In contrast the magnitude of this parameter in 2001 is 0,048. The taxable earnings of private firms were closer to income before taxes in 2002 than in 2001. The difference is statistically significant at the 1% level. In contrast, the financial and tax alignment of public firms was lower in 2002, however the difference is not statistically significant. The evidence suggests that public firms do not take (more) conforming book-tax positions after the new tax law was passed.[87]

Table 19: Regression results for differences in tax management levels between 2001 and 2002

		Expected sign	Model 1: Sub-sample of private firms estimated coefficients (*z-statistic/p-value*)	Model 2: Private versus public firms estimated coefficients (*z-statistic/p-value*)
Intercept	α_0	?	-0,483 *(-3,41/0,00)*	-0,426 *(-3,03/0,00)*
ΔWC	α_1	-	-7,846 *(-5,77/0,00)*	-8,093 *(-5,84/0,00)*
CFOP	α_2	-	-7,770 *(-5,60/0,00)*	-8,023 *(-5,66/0,00)*
MTR	α_3	+	1,250 *(8,98/0,00)*	1,188 *(8,86/0,00)*
YEAR	α_4	?	0,168 *(1,10/0,27)*	0,103 *(0,69/0,49)*
MTR*YEAR	α_5	?	-0,221 *(-1,10/0,27)*	-0,124 *(-0,63/0,53)*
PUBLIC	α_6	?	-	0,296 *(1,25/0,21)*
MTR*YEAR*PUBLIC	α_7	-	-	-0,687 *(-1,81/0,07)*
Sample size			1259	1327
Pseudo R^2			0,37	0,37
Wald χ^2 (p-value)			156,22 *(0,00)*	156,44 *(0,00)*

Results of the probit analysis. Dependent variable: EM is earnings management indicator variable, taking the value of 1 if the firm's earnings observation is in the first positive interval and 0 for all other intervals to the right of zero. Independent variables: ΔWC is changes in working capital computed as changes in current assets less changes in cash minus changes in current liabilities less changes in shot-term debt (scaled by lagged total assets); CFOP is cash flow from operations computed as operating income less changes in working capital (scaled by lagged total assets); MTR is marginal tax rate, a binary variable equalling 1 if the firm's marginal tax rate is equal or higher than the top statutory tax rate and 0 otherwise; PUBLIC is a public dummy, a binary variable equalling 1 for public firms and 0 for private firms and YEAR is a year dummy, a binary variable equalling 1 for the year 2002 and 0 for the year 2001.

[87] No comparative tests will be performed on the extent of book-tax differences between public and private firms. One reason for book-tax differences is accrual management. Taking different accrual positions for tax and financial accounting will increase the gap between the book and tax income. Russian private companies are expected to be more engaged in fraud accounting, while Russian public companies rather engage in accrual management. If public companies are at least to some extent interested in the reduction of taxes, then book-tax conformity of public firms may be even higher than of private firms.

Multivariate tests are performed next to assess the level of the difference in tax management between 2001 and 2002. The analysis begins with the sub-sample of private firms. Two additional variables are added into the model (64): a dummy variable YEAR equalling 1 for year 2002 and 0 for year 2001; and the interaction term of YEAR and MTR. No prediction is made about the sign on YEAR. If the new tax law changed reporting practices of Russian private firms, then the coefficient on the interaction term will be negative.

Table 19 shows the results for the multivariate probit analysis. Model 1 shows that results of the multivariate analysis are generally consistent with the results of univariate tests. The coefficient on the interaction term is negative but not significant. In the absence of demand for accounting information and by the lax tax enforcement, the change in the tax law results in no change in the level of tax management. Strong incentives for tax management of Russian private firms win over motivations to report earnings for valuation and monitoring purposes.

Table 19 (Model 2) reports the results of multivariate analysis for the effects of the changing reporting environment for the whole sample. We add PUBLIC and the interaction term MTR*PUBLIC*YEAR to assess whether the extent of tax management decreased in 2002 for Russian public firms. The coefficient on the interaction term is negative and significant (on the 10% level). This indicates that Russian public firms altered their behaviour in 2002 when they are faced with a stronger demand for accounting information, increasing tax enforcement and changing tax law.

4.5.5 SUMMARY FOR THE ROLE OF COMPETING INCENTIVES

Previous sections provided analysis of the effects of tax legislation on the earnings management behaviour of Russian private firms. The strong influence of tax legislation on the accounting regulation in the Russian Federation combined with the general "unwillingness" to pay taxes generated an environment in which one would hypothesize earnings management for the reduction of tax payments. Univariate tests showed a tendency of companies with high incentives for tax management to report unexpected large number of small profits. A multivariate analysis supported the results of the univariate tests. These findings are consistent with the hypothesis that companies manage earnings downwards to reduce tax expense.

Next the effect of reporting incentives on tax management by Russian firms is considered. It is hypothesized that the market pressure will create a reporting environment in which public firms are interested to report accounting data of a higher quality. Public companies are expected to be less aggressive tax managers because such reporting practices deteriorate earnings quality. The empirical results provide evidence for this prediction.

Further tests consider the effect of market forces, political enforcement and changing tax environment on reporting practices of private and public firms around the beginning of 2002. The demand for accounting information of private firms – which represents the influence of market forces – did not change during the period. The only users of accounting information of private companies over the whole observation period were the tax authorities. Accountants of private firms aligned the informativness of financial statements with the interests of the tax service. Political forces influenced through the tax enforcement that affected public and private firms to a different degree. Changing tax regulation brought significant changes into financial and tax alignment. Tax and financial reporting were separated from each other by the provisions of the Tax Code. Both univariate and multivariate tests showed results consistent with prior research on reporting incentives. In Russia the changing regulation *per se* did not have an observable effect on the extent of earnings management. After the new tax law was passed the informativeness of private firm earnings stayed constant. However the market and political pressure on public firms affected the extent of tax management of public firms. The extent of tax management of public companies in 2002 was smaller.

5 CONCLUSIONS

The purpose of the analysis was to analyse the determinants of earnings management. This was achieved (1) by providing an overview of the empirical research on factors that influence the extent of earnings management; and (2) by closing some gaps in this field of accounting research.

The first step of the analysis was to provide an overview of the results of the empirical research on earnings management motivations and constraints. Earnings management motivations are the factors that drive accounting choices and may increase the extent of earnings management. Earnings management constraints are the factors through which the demand for and/or supply of accounting information may inhibit earnings management practices. A particular feature (and actually a problem) of research in this area is an isolation of one single factor (i.e. a motivation or an environmental factor) that determines the extent of earnings management. This field of empirical research provided fruitful evidence on earnings management drivers and constraints. It was shown that the contractual, asset pricing and regulatory motivations drive accounting choice. Earnings management can be constrained either through the impact of market forces (i.e. demand constraints) or through the inhibitors on the supply of discretionary earnings (e.g., auditing, corporate governance, accounting standards and political enforcement). Empirical research on determinants of earnings management has several practical implications: First, it provides information for the users of financial statements on the quality of earnings that can be further used for e.g., business valuation. Second, it helps the law makers to enforce reporting of higher quality earnings.

Research on the motivations for earnings management identifies situations in which one can suspect earnings management. Examples include bonus contracts and debt covenants. The evidence on earnings management for contractual purposes exists since the middle of the 1980s. However, bonus contracts and debt covenants are still used by the major companies. There are two possible explanations for that: The rational explanation is that firms' stakeholders adjust their offering (e.g., the amount of bonus compensation or debt covenant) for earnings management. According to the irrational point of view, the stakeholders can be fooled by earnings management. In the presence of earnings management, contracts are still used because they are the best available instrument to solve the agency problem.

Despite the fact that it is not clear which of the explanations is correct, research on motivations for earnings management provides valuable insights for practitioners. While investors are (usually) treated as the rational market participants, no one denies that there are also some less sophisticated stakeholders that cannot undo the results of earnings management. For instance, research on the regulatory motivations for earnings management usually implies that it is too costly for state authorities to detect earnings management. As the research on motivations for earnings management identifies conditions under which earnings may be managed, this field of accounting research is of a primary interest to the users of financial statements. For the same reason research on motivations provides some valuable insights for the law makers: More direct enforcement actions can be taken when the situations under which earnings management occurs are known. Advances in two areas are necessary to facilitate the actions of stakeholders and the law makers: (1) detection techniques (to provide stakeholders with the tools for earnings management detection), and (2) research on more concrete motivations for earnings management. A good example is a study by Kasanen et al. (1996), which analyses earnings management to pay out the smooth dividend stream expected by the large institutional owners.

The extent of earnings management can be decreased if the earnings management constraints are strengthened. It was shown that earnings quality measured as earnings conservatism is a function of market forces.[88] Market demands accounting information of a high quality and penalises the companies that fail to do so. How well a market copes with this task depends on the stage of its development. Therefore, the regulatory actions that have the goal to improve the capital markets are also likely to constrain earnings management. Law makers may also turn to the supply-side constraints which are more easily to change. Improvements in the field of law enforcement will decrease the extent of earnings management. Both the shareholders and the law makers may also consider changing corporate governance structures and the audit quality to constrain income manipulations.

The overview showed that despite intensive research there are still some gaps in the analysis of earnings management constraints. For instance, it was theoretically demonstrated that accounting choices and that the costs of (accrual) earnings management are a function of latitude in accounting standards. However, empirical research failed to provide any evidence consistent with the crucial role of accounting rules. Chapter 4 showed that the accounting framework matters. Three competing accounting regimes were analysed on a single market: IAS/IFRS, German GAAP and U.S. GAAP. While the extent of earnings management under the former two accounting frameworks is roughly the same, it was shown that U.S. GAAP earnings are of a higher earnings quality. This has implications for standard setters. From a policy making perspective, the results can neither recommend nor discourage German lawmakers and regulators to allow the use of IAS/IFRS for company accounts or all types of groups, regardless of their use of capital markets. The data suggests that the level of earnings management will remain the same if IAS/IFRS do not converge towards U.S. GAAP.

The findings also suggest that the current improvement and convergence projects must be continued. U.S. GAAP seem to perform better than IAS/IFRS when institutional factors and economic incentives are the same.

The problem with the whole research on determinants of earnings management is the analysis of a one determinant at a time (i.e. there is usually a restriction to one single

[88] Empirical analysis in the fourth chapter supported these findings for earnings management.

factor). It is more likely that several factors determine the accounting choice: Several motivations as to e.g., report earnings above some threshold and to lower the present value of taxes are more likely to drive earnings management. Earnings management behaviour is then constrained by earnings management inhibitors each of which has its own unique impact on the extent of earnings quality. There are several ways to overcome the shortcomings of the present state of research. One is a more complicated statistical modelling (i.e. an estimation of simultaneous equation models is required). An example of such a research design is Beatty et al. (1995). The second way is to overcome the problems by a research design.

The second study in the fourth chapter uses a unique research sample to analyse the impact of a set of determinants on the extent of earnings management. The sample consists of observations of Russian private and public companies in years 2001 and 2002 (i.e. before and after the new law on income taxes was passed). Because of the number of motivations, from which tax minimization is the leading one, Russian companies opt to report managed earnings that are positive and very small in respect to the lagged total assets. Several factors constrain such behaviour: The demand for accounting information, which 'pushes' public firms to report earnings of a higher quality, and the tax enforcement, which mostly affects the large listed companies. The change in the financial and tax alignment in 2002 from high to low provided an option for firms to increase the quality of their earnings. In 2002 firms could separate financial and tax accounting and choose different accounting policies to calculate book and tax income. Results of both univariate and multivariate tests were consistent with the earnings management to reduce (the present value of) taxes. Further analysis showed that because of the impact of market and political forces public companies manage earnings (taxes) to a lesser extent than the private companies. The tests also revealed that the public firms exercised the regulatory option and increased the quality of reported earnings in 2002. Therefore, in Russia as in the other countries the changing regulation *per se* did not change the extent of earnings management. As a result the informativeness of private firm earnings stayed constant after the new tax law was passed. However the market and political pressure affected the extent of tax management of public firms. To promote the high quality financial reporting further reforms are necessary that will improve the functionality of the Russian capital market and increase the tax enforcement.

Further research may consider the incremental effect of several earnings management constraints and the substitution effect between them. An interesting question could be for example whether the lack of law enforcement on investor protection could be substituted by a 'good' corporate governance structure.

REFERENCES

ACFE, 1993, *Cooking the books: What every accountant should know about fraud* (No. 92-5401 Self-study workbook: 12).

AICPA, 1992, *Professional standards: Volume 1* (AICPA, New York).

Akerlof, George A., 1970, The market of 'lemons': quality uncertainty and the market mechanism, *Quarterly Journal of Economics* 90, 629-650.

Albrecht, W. David, and Frederick M. Richardson, 1990, Income smoothing by economy sector, *Journal of Business Finance and Accounting* 17, 713-730.

Ali, Ashiq, and Paul Zarowin, 1992, Permanent versus transitory components of annual earnings and estimation error in earnings response coefficients, *Journal of Accounting and Economics* 15, 286-296.

Antle, Rick, Elizabeth A. Gordon, Ganapathi Narayanamoorthy, and Ling Zhou, 2002, The joint determination of audit fees, non-audit fees, and abnormal accruals, Working paper, Yale University and Rutgers University.

Baginski, Stephen P., Keneth S. Lorek, G. Lee Willinger, and Bruce C. Branson, 1999, The relationship between economic characteristics and alternative annual earnings persistence measures, *The Accounting Review* 74, 105-120.

Bagnoli, Mark, and Susan G. Watts, 2000, The effect of relative performance evaluation on earnings management: a game-theoretic approach, *Journal of Accounting and Public Policy* 19, 377-397.

Bakaev, Alexander S., 2002, O nalogovom uchete i base ischisleniya dannyh dlya naloga na pribyl', *Buhgalterskij Uchet* 59-61.

Ball, Ray, and Philip Brown, 1968, An empirical evaluation of accounting income numbers, *Journal of Accounting Research* 6, 159-178.

Ball, Ray, and S.P. Kothari, 1991, Security returns around earnings announcements, *The Accounting Review* 66, 718-738.

Ball, Ray, S.P. Kothari, and Ashok Robin, 2000, The effect of international institutional factors on properties of accounting earnings, *Journal of Accounting and Economics* 29, 1-51.

Ball, Ray, Ashok Robin, and Joanna Shuang Wu, 2003, Incentives versus standards: Properties of accounting income in four East Asian countries, *Journal of Accounting and Economics* 36, 235-270.

Ball, Ray, and Lakshmanan Shivakumar, forthcoming, Earnings quality in UK private firms: Comparative loss recognition timeliness, *Journal of Accounting and Economics.*

Bange, Mary M., and Werner F.M. De Bondt, 1998, R&D budgets and corporate earnings targets, *Journal of Corporate Finance* 4, 153-184.

Barth, Mary E., William H. Beaver, and Wayne R. Landsman, 2001, The relevance of the value relevance literature for final accounting standard setting: Another view, *Journal of Accounting and Economics* 31, 77-104.

Barth, Mary E., John A. Elliott, and Mark W. Finn, 1999, Market rewards associated with patterns of increasing earnings, *Journal of Accounting Research* 37, 387-413.

Bartov, Eli, 1993, The timing of asset sales and earnings manipulation, *The Accounting Review* 68, 840-855.

Bartov, Eli, Stephen R. Goldberg, and Myung-Sun Kim, 2001, The valuation-relevance of earnings and cash flows: An international Perspective, *Journal of International Financial Management and Accounting* 12, 103-132.

Bartov, Eli, Stephen R. Goldberg, and Myung-Sun Kim, 2002, Comparative value relevance among German, U.S. and international accounting standards: A German stock market perspective, Working paper, New York University, Grand Valley State University and University of Missouri-Columbia.

Basu, Sudipta, 1997, The conservatism principle and the asymmetric timeliness of earnings, *Journal of Accounting and Economics* 24, 3-37.

Bauwhede, Heidi Vander, and Marleen Willekens, 2003, Earnings management in Belgium: a review of the empirical evidence, *Tijdschrift voor economie en management* 48, 199-217.

Bauwhede, Heidi Vander, Marleen Willekens, and Ann Gaeremynck, 2003, Audit firm size, public ownership, and firms' discretionary accruals management, *The International Journal of Accounting* 38, 1-22.

Beatty, Anne L., Sandra L. Chamberlain, and Joseph Magliolo, 1995, Managing financial reports of commercial banks: the influence of taxes, regulatory capital, and earnings, *Journal of Accounting Research* 33, 231-261.

Beatty, Anne L., and David G. Harris, 1999, The effects of taxes, agency costs and information asymmetry on earnings management: A comparison of public and private firms, *Review of Accounting Studies* 3, 299-326.

Beatty, Anne L., Bin Ke, and Kathy R. Petroni, 2002, Earnings management to avoid earnings declines across publicly and privately held banks, *The Accounting Review* 77, 547-570.

Beatty, Anne L., and Joseph Weber, 2003, The effects of debt contracting on voluntary accounting method changes, *The Accounting Review* 78, 119-142.

Beaver, William H., 1968, The information content of annual earnings announcements, *Journal of Accounting Research* 6, 67-92.

Beaver, William H., 2002, Perspectives on recent capital market research, *The Accounting Review* 77, 453-474.

Beaver, William H., and Ellen E. Engel, 1996, Discretionary behavior with respect to allowances for loan losses and the behavior of security prices, *Journal of Accounting and Economics* 22, 177-206.

Beaver, William H., Maureen F. McNichols, and Karen K. Nelson, 2003, Management of the loss reserve accrual and the distribution of earnings in the property-casualty insurance industry, *Journal of Accounting and Economics* 35, 347-376.

Beaver, William H., and Stephen G. Ryan, 2000, Biases and lags in book value and their effects on the ability of the book-to-market ratio to predict book return on equity, *Journal of Accounting Research* 38, 127-148.

Becker, Connie L., Mark L. DeFond, James Jiambalvo, and K.R. Subramanyam, 1998, The effect of audit quality on earnings management, *Contemporary Accounting Research* 15, 1-24.

Beekes, Wendy, 2003, Earnings management in response to regulatory price review. A case study of the political cost hypothesis in the water and electricity sectors in England and Wales, Working paper, University of Lancaster.

Beneish, Messod D., 1997, Detecting GAAP violation: implications for assessing earnings management among firms with extreme financial performance, *Journal of Accounting and Public Policy* 16, 271-309.

Benford, Frank, 1938, The law of anomalous numbers, *Proceedings of the American Philosophical Society* 78, 551-572.

Berle, Adolf A., and Gardiner C. Means, 1932, *The modern corporation and private property* (MacMillan, New York).

Bernard, Victor L., and Douglas J. Skinner, 1996, What motivates managers' choice of discretionary accruals? *Journal of Accounting and Economics* 22, 313-325.

Bhattacharya, Utpal, Hazem Daouk, and Michael Welker, 2003, The world price of earnings opacity, *The Accounting Review* 78, 641-678.

Biggs, Stanley F., and John J. Wild, 1984, A note on the practice of analytical review, *Auditing* 3, 68-79.

Black, Ervin L., Keith F. Sellers, and Tracy S. Manly, 1998, Earnings management using asset sales: An international study of countries allowing non-current asset revaluation, *Journal of Business Finance and Accounting* 25, 1287-1317.

Born, Karl, 2001a, *Bilanzanalyse international*, Second Edition, (Schäffer-Poeschel, Stuttgart, Germany).

Born, Karl, 2001b, *Rechnungslegung nach IAS, U.S. GAAP und HGB im Vergleich* (Schäffer-Poeschel, Stuttgart, Germany).

Botosan, Christine A., and Carol A. Frost, 1998, Regulation, disclosure and market liquidity: An examination of foreign issuers in regulated versus less regulated U.S. equity markets, Working paper, University of Utah and Washington University.

Bowen, Robert M. David Burgstahler, and Lane A. Daley, 1987, The incremental information content of accrual versus cash flows, *The Accounting Review* 62, 723-747.

Boynton, Charles E., Paul S. Dobbins, and George A. Plesko, 1992, Earnings management and the corporate alternative minimum tax, *Journal of Accounting Research* 30, 131-153.

Bradshaw, Mark T., and Richard G. Sloan, 2002, GAAP versus the street: An empirical assessment of two alternative definitions of earnings, *Journal of Accounting Research* 40, 41-66.

Brown, Lawrence D., and Kumar N. Sivakumar, 2001, Comparing the quality of three earnings measures, Working paper, Georgia State University and Boston University.

Buijink, Willem, Laurent Coppens, and Erik Peek, 2004, Accounting conservatism in the European Union: The influence of incentives, regulation and enforcement, Working paper, Tilburg University and Universiteit Maastricht.

Burgstahler. David, and Ilia Dichev, 1997, Earnings management to avoid earnings decreases and losses, *Journal of Accounting and Economics* 24, 99-126.

Burgstahler, David, Luzi Hail, and Christian Leuz, 2004, The importance of reporting incentives: Earnings management in European private and public firms, Working paper, University of Washington/Seattle, University of Zurich and University of Pennsylvania.

Cahan, Stven F., 1992, The effect of antitrust investigations on discretionary accruals: A refined test of the political-cost hypothesis, *The Accounting Review* 67, 77-95.

Calderon, Thomas G., and Brian P. Green, 1994, Signalling fraud by using analytical procedures, *The Ohio CPA Journal* 27-38.

Carslaw, Charles A.P.N., 1988, Anomalies in income numbers: Evidence of goal oriented behavior, *The Accounting Review* 63, 321-327.

Chambers, Dennis J., 1999, Earnings management and capital market misallocation, Working paper, University of Illionois at Urbana-Champaign.

Christie, Andrew A., and Jerold L. Zimmerman, 1994, Efficient and opportunistic choices of accounting procedures: corporate control contests, *The Accounting Review* 69, 539-566.

Chung, Richard, Michael Firth, and Jeong-Bon Kim, 2002, Institutional monitoring and opportunistic earnings management, *Journal of Corporate Finance* 8, 29-48.

Cloyd, C. Bryan, Jamie Pratt, and Toby Stock, 1996, The use of financial accounting choice to support aggressive tax positions: public and private firms, *Journal of Accounting Research* 34, 23-43.

Collingwood, Harris, 2001, The earnings game, *Harvard Business Review* 79, 65-74.

Collins, Daniel W., and S.P. Kothari, 1989, An analysis of inter-temporal and cross-sectional determinants of earnings response coefficients, *Journal of Accounting and Economics* 11, 143-181.

Copeland, Ronald M., 1968, Income smoothing, *Journal of Accounting Research* 6, 101-116.

Coppens, Laurent, and Erik Peek, 2004, An analysis of earnings management by European private firms, Working paper, Netmanagement Reseaux Bruxelles/Netten Brussel and University Maastricht.

Cornell, Bradford, and Alan C. Shapiro, 1987, Corporate stakeholders and corporate finance, *Financial Management* 16, 5-14.

Cushing, Barry E., and Marc J. LeClere, 1992, Evidence on the determinants of inventory accounting policy, *The Accounting Review* 67, 355-366.

Daley, Lane A., and Robert L. Vigeland, 1983, The effects of debt covenants and political costs on the choice of accounting methods: The case of accounting for R&D costs, *Journal of Accounting and Economics* 5, 195-211.

Daroca, Frank P., and William W. Holder, 1985, The use of analytical procedures in review and audit engagements, *Auditing* 4, 80-92.

Das, Somnath, and Huai Zhang, 2000, Rounding-up in reported EPS, behavioral thresholds, and earnings management, Working paper, University of Illinois.

Das, Somnath, and Huai Zhang, 2003, Rounding-up an reported EPS, behavioral thresholds, and earnings management, *Journal of Accounting and Economics* 35, 31-50.

DeAngelo, Harry, Linda DeAngelo, and Douglas J. Skinner, 1994, Accounting choice in troubled companies, *Journal of Accounting and Economics* 17, 113-143.

DeAngelo, Harry, Linda DeAngelo, and Douglas J. Skinner, 1996, Reversal of future dividend signalling and the disappearance of sustained earnings growth, *Journal of Financial Economics* 40, 341-371.

DeAngelo, Linda, 1986, Accounting numbers as market valuation substitutes: a study of management buyouts of public stockholders, *The Accounting Review* 61, 400-420.

DeAngelo, Linda E., 1981, Auditor size and audit quality, *Journal of Accounting and Economics* 3, 183-199.

Dechow, Patricia M., 1994, Accounting earnings and cash flows as measures of firm performance. The role of accounting accruals, *Journal of Accounting and Economics* 18, 3-42.

Dechow, Patricia M., and Ilia D. Dichev, 2002, The quality of accruals and earnings: The role of accrual estimation errors, *The Accounting Review* 77, 35-70.

Dechow, Patricia M., Amy P. Hutton, and Richard G. Sloan, 1999, An empirical assessment of the residual income valuation model, *Journal of Accounting and Economics* 26, 1-34.

Dechow, Patricia M., S.P. Kothari, and Ross L. Watts, 1998, The relation between earnings and cash flows, *Journal of Accounting and Economics* 25, 133-168.

Dechow, Patricia M., Scott A. Richardson, and A. Irem Tuna, 2003, Why are earnings kinky? An examination of the earnings management explanation, *Review of Accounting Studies* 8, 355-384.

Dechow, Patricia M., and Douglas J. Skinner, 2000, Earnings management: reconciling the views of accounting academics, practitioners, and regulators, *Accounting Horizons* 14, 235-250.

Dechow, Patricia M., and Richard G. Sloan, 1991, Executive incentives and the horizon problem, *Journal of Accounting and Economics* 14, 51-89.

Dechow, Patricia M., Richard G. Sloan, and Amy P. Sweeney, 1995, Detecting Earnings Management, *The Accounting Review* 70, 193-225.

Dechow, Patricia M., Richard G. Sloan, and Amy P. Sweeney, 1996, Causes and consequences of earnings manipulation: An analysis of firm subject to enforcement actions by the SEC, *Contemporary Accounting Research* 13, 1-36.

DeFond, Mark L., and James Jiambalvo, 1994, Debt covenant violation and manipulation of accruals, *Journal of Accounting and Economics* 17, 145-176.

DeFond, Mark L., and Chul W. Park, 1997, Smoothing income in anticipation of future earnings, *Journal of Accounting and Economics* 23, 115-139.

DeFond, Mark L., and Chul W. Park, 2001, The reversal of abnormal accruals and the market valuation of earnings surprises, *The Accounting Review* 76, 375-404.

DeFond, Mark L., and K.R. Subramanyam, 1998, Auditor changes and discretionary accruals, *Journal of Accounting and Economics* 25, 35-67.

Degeorge, Francois, Jayendu Patel, and Richard Zeckhauser, 1999, Earnings management to exees thresholds, *Journal of Business* 72, 1-33.

Demski, Joel S., 1998, Performance measure manipulation, *Contemporary Accounting Research* 15, 261-285.

Desai, Mihir A., Alexander Dyck, and Luigi Zingales, 2003, The protecting hand: taxation and corporate governance, Working paper, Harvard University and University of Chicago.

Dichev, Ilia D., and Douglas J. Skinner, 2002, Large-sample evidence on the debt covenant hypothesis, *Journal of Accounting Research* 40, 1091-1123.

Durtschi, Cindy, and Peter D. Easton, 2004, Earnings management? Alternative explanations for observed discontinuities in the frequency distribution of earnings, earnings changes, and analyst forecast errors, Working paper, Utah State University and University of Notre Dame.

Dyck, Alexander, and Luigi Zingales, 2004, Private benefits of control: An international comparison, *The Journal of Finance* 59, 537-600.

Dye, Ronald A., and Shyam Sunder, 2001, Why not allow FASB and IASB, *standards to compete in the U.S.* 15, 257-271.

Easterwood, Cintia M., 1997/1998, Takeovers and incentives for earnings management: An empirical analysis, *Journal of Applied Business Research* 14, 29-47.

Easton, Peter D., Trevor S. Harris, and James A. Ohlson, 1992, Aggregate accounting earnings can explain most of security returns: the case of long event windows, *Journal of Accounting and Economics* 15, 119-142.

Easton, Peter D., and Mark E. Zmijewski, 1989, Cross-sectional variation in the stock market response to accounting earnings announcements, *Journal of Accounting and Economics* 11, 117-141.

Elliott, John A., and Wayne H. Shaw, 1988, Write-offs as accounting procedures to manage perceptions, *Journal of Accounting Research* 26, 91-119.

Erickson, Merle M., and Shiing-wu Wang, 1999, Earnings management by acquiring firms in stock for stock mergers, *Journal of Accounting and Economics* 27, 149-176.

Ewert, Ralf, and Alfred Wagenhofer, 2004, Economic effects of tightening accounting standards to restrict earnings management, Working paper, J.W. Goete-Universität Frankfurt am Main and University of Graz.

Fama, Eugene F., and Michael C. Jensen, 1983a, Separation of ownership and control, *Journal of Law and Economics* 26, 301-325.

Fama, Eugene F., and Michael C. Jensen, 1983b, Agency problems and residual claims, *Journal of Law and Economics* 26, 327-349.

Feltham, Gerald A., and James A. Ohlson, 1995, Valuation and clean surplus accounting for operating and financial activities, *Contemporary Accounting Research* 11, 689-731.

Feltham, Gerald A., and James A. Ohlson, 1996, Uncertainty resolution and the theory of depreciation measurement, *Journal of Accounting Research* 34, 209-234.

Fields, Thomas D., Thomas Z. Lys, and Linda Vincent, 2001, Empirical research on accounting choice, *Journal of Accounting and Economics* 31, 255-307.

Fischer, Paul E., and Robert E. Verrecchia, 2000, Reporting bias, *The Accounting Review* 75, 229-245.

Francis, Jennifer, 2001, Discussion of empirical research on accounting choice, *Journal of Accounting and Economics* 31, 309-319.

Francis, Jennifer, Ryan LaFond, Per Olsson, and Katherine Schipper, 2003, Costs of capital and earnings attributes, Working paper, Duke University, University of Wisconsin and FASB.

Francis, Jennifer, Robert Lipe, Per Olsson, and Katherine Schipper, 2002, The market pricing of earnings quality, Working paper, Duke University, University of Wisconsin and FASB.

Francis, Jere R., J. Douglas Hanna, and Linda Vincent, 1996, Causes and effects of discretionary assets write-offs, *Journal of Accounting Research* 34, 117-134.

Francis, Jere R., Edward L. Maydew, and Charles H. Sparks, 1999, The role of Big 6 auditors in the credible reporting of accruals, *Auditing: A Journal of Practice & Theory* 18, 17-34.

Fudenberg, Drew, and Jean Tirole, 1995, A theory of income and dividend smoothing based on incumbency rents, *Journal of Political Economy* 103, 75-93.

Garcia Lara, Juan Manuel, Beatriz Garcia Osma, and Araceli Mora, 2003, The effect of earnings management on the asymmetric timeliness of earnings, Working paper, Lancaster University and Universidad de Valincia.

Garza-Gomez, Xavier, Masashi Okumura, and Michio Kunimura, 1999, Discretionary accruals model and the accounting process, Working paper, Nagoya City University.

Gaver, Jennifer J., and Jeffrey S. Paterson, 2004, Do insurers manipulate loss reserves to mask solvency problems? *Journal of Accounting and Economics* 37, 393-416.

Giroux, Gary, 2004, *Detecting earnings management* (John Wiley & Sons, Inc., Hoboken, NJ).

Givoly, Dan, and Carla Hayn, 2000, The changing time-series properties of earnings, cash flows and accruals: Has financial reporting become more conservative? *Journal of Accounting and Economics* 29, 287-320.

Givoly, Dan, and Joshua Ronen, 1981, 'Smoothing' manifestations in fourth quarter results of operations: some empirical evidence, *Abacus* 17, 174-193.

Goncharov, Igor and Jochen Zimmermann, 2003, Do Accounting Standards Influence the Level of Earnings Management? Evidence from Germany, Working paper, LBS Accounting Subject Area Working Paper ACCT041.

Goncharov, Igor and Jochen Zimmermann, 2004, Earnings Management when Incentives Compete: The Role of Tax Accounting in Russia, Working paper, University of Bremen.

Gorbatova, L., 2000, Reforma buhgalterskogo ucheta glazami ekonomista, *Voprosy Ekonomiki,* 103-112.

Gore, Pelham, Peter Pope, and Ashni Singh, 2002, Earnings management and the distribution of earnings relative to targets: UK evidence, Working paper, Lancaster University.

Gramlich, Jeffrey D., 1991, The effect of the alternative minimum tax book income adjustment on accrual decisions, *The Journal of the American Taxation Association* 13, 36-56.

Gray, Sidney J., 1988, Towards a theory of cultural influence on the development of accounting systems internationally, *Abacus* 24, 1-15.

Green, Brian Patrick, and Jae Hwa Choi, 1997, Assessing the risk of management fraud through neural network technology, *Auditing* 16, 14-28.

Guan, Liming, and Hamid Pourjalali, 2003, Effects of cultural environment and accounting regulation on earnings management: A multiple year-country analysis, Working paper, University of Havaii at Manoa.

Guay, Wayne R., S.P. Kothari, and Ross L. Watts, 1996, A market-based evaluation of discretionary accruals models, *Journal of Accounting Research* 34, 83-105.

Guenther, David A., 1994, Earnings management in response to corporate tax rate changes: Evidence from the 1986 Tax Reform Act, *Journal of Accounting Research* 69, 230-243.

Guidry, Flora, Andrew J. Leone, and Steve Rock, 1999, Earnings-based bonus plans and earnings management by business-unit managers, *Journal of Accounting and Economics* 26, 113-142.

Hall, Steven C., and William W. Stammerjohan, 1997, Damage awards and earnings management in the oil industry, *The Accounting Review* 72, 47-65.

Hall, Steven C., and William W. Stammerjohan, 2003, Legal costs and accounting choices: Another test of the litigation hypothesis, *Journal of Business Finance and Accounting* 30, 829-862.

Han, Jerry D.Y., and Shiing-wu Wang, 1998, Political costs and earnings management of oil companies during the 1990 Persian Gulf crisis, *The Accounting Review* 73, 103-117.

Hand, John R.M., and Terrance R. Skantz, 1998, The economic determinants of accounting choice: The unique case of equity carve-outs under SAB 51, *Journal of Accounting and Economics* 24, 175-203.

Harris, Trevor S., Mark Lang, and Hans Peter Möller, 1994, The value relevance of German accounting measures: An empirical analysis, *Journal of Accounting Research* 32, 187-209.

Hayn, Carla, 1995, The information content of losses, *Journal of Accounting and Economics* 20, 125-153.

Healy, Paul M., 1985, The effect of bonus schemes on accounting decisions, *Journal of Accounting and Economics* 7, 85-107.

Healy, Paul M., and Krishna G. Palepu, 1990, Earnings and risk changes surrounding primary stock offers, *Journal of Accounting Research* 28, 25-48.

Healy, Paul M., and Krishna G. Palepu, 2001, Information asymmetry, corporate disclosure, and the capital markets: A review of the empirical disclosure literature, *Journal of Accounting and Economics* 31, 405-440.

Healy, Paul M., and James M. Wahlen, 1999, A review of the earnings management literature and its implications for standard setting, *Accounting Horizons* 13, 365-383.

Herrmann, Don, Tatsuo Inoue, and Wayne B. Thomas, 2003, The sales of assets to manage earnings in Japan, *Journal of Accounting Research* 41, 89-108.

Hicks, John R., 1939, *Value and capital* (University Press, Oxford, U.K.).

Hofstede, Geert, 1980, *Culture's consequences: International differences in work-related values. Integral edition* (Sage, Beverly Hills, CA; London, U.K.; New Dehli, India).

Hofstede, Geert, 1983, Cultural dimensions for project management, *International Journal of Project Management* 1, 41-48.

Holthausen, Robert W., 1981, Evidence on the effect of bond covenants and management compensation contracts on the choice of accounting techniques: The case of the depreciation switch-back, *Journal of Accounting and Economics* 3, 73-109.

Holthausen, Robert W., 1990, Accounting method choice: Opportunistic behavior, efficient contracting, and information perspectives, *Journal of Accounting and Economics* 12, 207-218.

Holthausen, Robert W., 2003, Testing the relative power of accounting standards versus incentives and other institutional features to influence the outcome of financial reporting in an international setting, *Journal of Accounting and Economics* 36, 271-283.

Holthausen, Robert W., David F. Larcker, and Richard G. Sloan, 1995, Annual bonus schemes and the manipulation of earnings, *Journal of Accounting and Economics* 19, 29-74.

Holthausen, Robert W., and Ross L. Watts, 2001, The relevance of the value-relevance literature for financial accounting standard setting, *Journal of Accounting and Economics* 31, 3-75.

Iniguez, Raul, and Francisco Poveda, 2004, Long-run abnormal returns and income smoothing in the Spanish stock market, *European Accounting Review* 13, 105-130.

Jensen, Gerald R., Donald P. Soldberg, and Thomas S. Zorn, 1992, Simultaneous determination of insider ownership, debt, and dividend policies, *Journal of Financial and Quantitative Analysis* 27, 247-263.

Jensen, Michael C., 1986, Agency costs of free cash flow, *The American Economic Review* 76, 323-329.

Jensen, Michael C., 1993, The modern industrial revolution, exit, and the failure of internal control systems, *The Journal of Finance* 48, 831-880.

Jensen, Michael C., and William H. Meckling, 1976, Theory of the firm: Managerial behavior, agency costs and ownership structure, *Journal of Financial Economics* 3, 305-360.

Jeter, Debra C., and Lakshmanan Shivakumar, 1999, Cross-sectional estimation of abnormal accruals using quarterly and annual data: Effectiveness in detecting event-specific earnings management, *Accounting and Business Research* 29, 299-319.

Johnson, W. Bruce, and Ramachandran Ramanan, 1988, Discretionary accounting changes from "successful efforts" to "full cost" methods: 1970-76, *The Accounting Review* 63, 96-110.

Jones, Jennifer J., 1991, Earnings management during import relief investigations, *Journal of Accounting Research* 29, 193-228.

Kamin, Jacob Y., and Joshua Ronen, 1978, The effects of corporate control on apparent profit performance, *Southern Economic Journal* 45, 181-191.

Kang, Sok-Hyon, 1999, A conceptual and empirical evolution of accrual prediction models, Working paper, Yale School of Management.

Kang, Sok-Hyon, and K. Sivaramakrishnan, 1995, Issues in testing earnings management and an instrumental variable approach, *Journal of Accounting Research* 33, 353-367.

Kaplan, Robert S., 1985, Comments on Paul Healy: Evidence on the effect of bonus schemes on accounting procedure and accrual decisions, *Journal of Accounting and Economics* 7, 109-113.

Kasanen, Eero, Juha Kinnunen, and Jyrki Niskanen, 1996, Dividend-based earnings management: empirical evidence from Finland, *Journal of Accounting and Economics* 22, 283-312.

Kasznik, Ron, 1999, On the association between voluntary disclosure and earnings management, *Journal of Accounting Research* 37, 57-81.

Keating, A. Scott, and Jerold L. Zimmerman, 2000, Depreciation-policy changes: tax, earnings management, and investment opportunity incentives, *Journal of Accounting and Economics* 28, 359-389.

Key, Kimberly Galligan, 1997, Political cost incentives for earnings management in the cable television industry, *Journal of Accounting and Economics* 23, 309-337.

Kinnunen, Juha, and Markku Koskela, 2003, Who is miss world in cosmetic earnings management? A cross-national comparison of small upwards rounding in net income numbers among eighteen countries, *Journal of International Accounting Research* 2, 39-68.

Klein, April, 2002, Audit committee, board of director characteristics, and earnings management, *Journal of Accounting and Economics* 33, 375-400.

Klyamkin, Igor M., and Lev M. Timofeev, 2000, *Tenevaya Rossiya* (Rossijskij Gosudarstvennyj Gumanitarnyj Institut, Moscow, Russia).

Knechel, W. Robert, 1986, A summary study of the relative effectiveness of alternative analytical review procedures, *Decision Sciences* 17, 376-394.

Koch, Bruce S., 1981, Income smoothing: An experiment, *The Accounting Review* 56, 574-586.

Koch, Timothy W., and Larry D. Wall, 2000, Bank loan-loss accounting: a review of theoretical and empirical evidence, *Economic Review (Federal Reserve Bank of Atlanta)* 85, 1-19.

Kormendi, Roger, and Robert Lipe, 1987, Earnings innovations, earnings persistence, and stock returns, *Journal of Business* 60, 323-345.

Kothari, S.P., 2001, Capital market research in accounting, *Journal of Accounting and Economics* 31, 105-231.

Kothari, S.P., Andrew J. Leone, and Charles E. Wasley, 2002, Performance matched discretionary accrual measures, Working paper, University of Rochester.

Kothari, S.P., and Jerold L. Zimmerman, 1995, Price and return models, *Journal of Accounting and Economics* 20, 155-192.

Krishnan, Gopal V., 2003, Does Big 6 auditor industry expertise constrain earnings management? *Accounting Horizons* 17, 1-16.

La Porta, Rafael, Florencio Lopez-de-Silanes, Andrei Shleifer, and Robert W. Vishny, 2000, Investor protection and corporate governance, *Journal of Financial Economics* 58, 3-27.

La Porta, Rafael, Florencio Lopez-de-Silanes, Andrei Shleifer, and Robert W. Vishny, 1998, Law and finance, *Journal of Political Economy* 106, 1113-1155.

Lachnit, Laurenz, 2004, *Bilanzanalyse* (Gabler, Wiesbaden, Germany).

Lamb, Margaret, Christopher Nobes, and Alan Roberts, 1998, International variations in the connections between tax and financial reporting, *Accounting and Business Research* 28, 173-188.

Landsman, Wayne R., and Joseph Magliolo, 1988, Cross-sectional capital market research and model specification, *The Accounting Review* 63, 586-604.

Lang, Mark, Jana Smith Raedy, and Wendy Wilson, 2004, Earnings management and cross listing: Are reconciled earnings comparable to U.S. earnings? Working paper, University of North Carolina.

Larcker, David F., and Scott A. Richardson, 2003, Corporate governance, fees for non-audit services and accrual choices, Working paper, University of Pennsylvania.

Ledeneva, Alena V., and Marina Kurkchiyan, eds., 2000, *Economic Crime in Russia* (Kluwer Law International, The Hague, The Netherlands).

Leuz, Christian, 2003, IAS versus U.S. GAAP: Information asymmetry-based evidence from Germany's new market, *Journal of Accounting Research* 41, 445-472.

Leuz, Christian, Dhananjay Nanda, and Peter D. Wysocki, 2003, Earnings management and investors protection: An international comparison, *Journal of Financial Economics* 69, 505-527.

Lev, Baruch, 1983, Some economic determinants of time-series properties of earnings, *Journal of Accounting and Economics* 5, 31-48.

Lev, Baruch, and Doron Nissim, 2002, Taxable income as an indicator of earnings quality, Working paper, New York University and Columbia University.

Levitt, Arthur Jr., 1998, The 'numbers game', *CPA Journal* 68, 14-19.

Liesman, Steve, and Jonathan Weil, 2001, Corporate-profits miracle of 1990s loses luster over big write-offs, *The Wall Street Journal Europe* 19, 11 July 2001.

Lilien, Steven, and Victor Pastena, 1982, Determinants of intra-method choice in the oil and gas industry, *Journal of Accounting and Economics* 4, 145-170.

Lipe, Robert, 1990, The relation between stock returns and accounting earnings given alternative information, *The Accounting Review* 65, 49-71.

Liu, Chi-Chun, and Stephen G. Ryan, 1995, The effect of bank loan portfolio composition on the market reaction to and anticipation of loan loss provisions, *Journal of Accounting Research* 33, 77-94.

Liu, Chi-Chun, Stephen G. Ryan, and James M. Wahlen, 1997, Differential valuation implications of loan loss provisions across banks and fiscal quarters, *The Accounting Review* 72, 133-146.

Lougee, Barbara A., and Carol A. Marquardt, 2004, Earnings informativeness and strategic disclosure: an empirical examination of "pro forma" earnings, *The Accounting Review* 79, 769-795.

Magnan, Michel, Cathy Nadeau, and Denis Cormier, 1999, Earnings management during antidumping investigations: analysis and implications, *Canadian Journal of Administrative Sciences* 16, 149-162.

Makar, Stephen D., Pervaiz Alam, and Michael A. Peasrson, 1998, Antitrust merger investigations and the quality of reported earnings, *The Journal of Applied Business Research* 14, 89-100.

Maksimovic, Vojislav, and Sheridan Titman, 1991, Financial policy and reputation for product quality, *Review of Financial Studies* 4, 175-200.

Manzon, Gil B., Jr., 1992, Earnings management of firms subject to the alternative minimum tax, *Journal of the American Taxation Association* 14, 88-111.

Marquardt, Carol A., and Cristine I. Wiedman, 2004, The effect of earnings management on the value relevance of accounting information, *Journal of Business Finance and Accounting* 31, 297-332.

Maydew, Edward L., 1997, Tax-induced earnings management by firms with net operating losses, *Journal of Accounting Research* 35, 83-96.

McNichols, Maureen F., 2000, Research design issues in earnings management studies, *Journal of Accounting and Public Policy* 19, 313-345.

McNichols, Maureen F., and G. Peter Wilson, 1988, Evidence of earnings management from the provision for bad debts, *Journal of Accounting Research* 26, 1-31.

Meitner, Matthias, Felix Hüfner, and Volker Kleff, 2002, Enron: Wirtschaftsprüfer, Bilanzierungsvortschriften und der deutsche Aktienmarkt, *Zeitschrift für kapitalmarktorientierte Rechnungslegung* 2, 139-141.

Mendenhall, Richard R., and William D. Nichols, 1988, Bad news and differential market reactions to announcements of earlier-quarters versus fourth-quarter earnings, *Journal of Accounting Research* 26, 63-86.

Menges, Guenter, 1968, *Grungriss der Statistik Teil 1: Theorie* (Westdeutsche Verlag, Cologne, Germany).

Mikhail, Michael B., 1999, Coordination of earnings, regulatory capital and taxes in private and public companies, Working paper, Duke University.

Mills, Lillian F., and Kaye J. Newberry, 2001, The influence of tax and non-tax costs on book-tax reporting differences: public and private firms, *The Journal of the American Taxation Association* 23, 1-19.

Moses, O. Douglas, 1987, Income Smoothing and Incentives: Empirical Tests Using Accounting Changes, *The Accounting Review* 62, 358-377.

Moyer, Susan E., 1990, Capital adequacy ratio regulations and accounting choices in commercial banks, *Journal of Accounting and Economics* 13, 123-154.

Müller, Stefan, and Inge Wulf, 2001, Jahresabschlusspolitik nach HGB, IAS und U.S. GAAP, *Bilanzrecht und Wirtschaftsprüfung* 56, 2206-2213.

Murphy, Kevin J., and Jerold L. Zimmerman, 1993, Financial performance surrounding CEO turnover, *Journal of Accounting and Economics* 16, 273-315.

Myers, James N., 1999, Implementing residual income valuation with linear information dynamics, *The Accounting Review* 74, 1-28.

Myers, James N., Linda A. Myers, and Thomas C. Omer, 2003, Exploring the term of the auditor-client relationship and the quality of reported earnings: A case for mandatory auditor rotation? *The Accounting Review* 78, 779-799.

Navissi, Farshid, 1999, Earnings management under price regulation, *Contemporary Accounting Research* 16, 281-304.

Nelson, Mark W., John A. Elliott, and Robin L. Tarpley, 2003, How are earnings managed? Examples from auditors, *Accounting Horizons* 17, 17-35.

Peasnell, Ken V., Peter F. Pope, and Steven Young, 2000, Board monitoring and earnings management: Do outside directors influence abnormal accruals? Working paper, Lancaster University.

Peasnell, Ken V., Peter F. Pope, and Steven Young, 2000, Detecting earnings management using cross-sectional abnormal accruals models, *Accounting and Business Research* 30, 313-326.

Penman, Stephen, 2001, *Financial statement analysis and security valuation* (McGraw Hill/Irwin, New York, NY).

Penman, Stephen H., and Xiao-Jun Zhang, 2002, Accounting conservatism, the quality of earnings, and stock returns, *The Accounting Review* 77, 237-264.

Perry, Susan E., and Thomas H. Williams, 1994, Earnings management preceding management buyout offers, *Journal of Accounting and Economics* 18, 157-179.

Petroni, Kathy R., 1992, Optimistic reporting in the property-casualty insurance industry, *Journal of Accounting and Economics* 15, 485-508.

Petroni, Kathy R., Stephen G. Ryan, and James M. Wahlen, 2000, Discretionary and non-discretionary revisions of loss reserves by property-casualty insurers: Differential implications for future profitability, risk and market value, *Review of Accounting Studies* 5, 95-125.

Phillips, John, Morton Pincus, and Sonja Olhoft Rego, 2003, Earnings management: New evidence based on deferred tax expense, *The Accounting Review* 78, 491-521.

Pincus, Morton, and Shivaram Rajgopal, 2002, The interaction between accrual management and hedging: Evidence from oil and gas firms, *The Accounting Review* 77, 127-160.

Pourciau, Susan, 1993, Earnings management and nonroutine executive changes, *Journal of Accounting and Economics* 16.

Pownall, Grace, and Katherine Schipper, 1999, Implications of accounting research for the SEC's consideration of International Accounting Standards for U.S. securities offerings, *Accounting Horizons* 13, 259-280.

Preobragenskaya, Galina G., and Robert W. McGee, 2004, Converting the accounting system of a transition economy: A case study of Russia, Working paper, Barry University.

PricewaterhouseCoopers, 2003a, PricewaterhouseCoopers securities litigation study, Available at: http://www.10b5.com/.

PricewaterhouseCoopers, 2003b, PricewaterhouseCoopers Foreign Securities Litigation Study, Available at: http://www.10b5.com/.

Prokop, Jörg, 2003, *Die Bewertung zukünftiger Unternehmenserfolge. Konzepte - Möglichkeiten - Grenzen* (Deutscher Universitäts-Verlag, Wiesbaden, Germany).

Radaev, Vadim, 2002, Rossijskij business: na puti k legalizacii? *Voprosy Ekonomiki,* 68-87.

Rangan, Srinivasan, 1998, Earnings management and the performance of seasoned equity offerings, *Journal of Financial Economics* 50, 101-122.

Revsine, Lawrence, Daniel W. Collins, and W. Bruce Johnson, 2002. *Financial Reporting and Analysis* (Pearson Education Inc., Upper Sadle River, NJ).

Richardson, Scott A., 2003, Earnings quality and short sellers, *Accounting Horizons* 17, 49-61.

Roychowdhury, Sugata, 2004, Management of earnings through the manipulation of real activities that effect cash flow from operations, Working paper, MIT.

Rozhnova, Olga, 2000, The problem of perception of the new Russian Accounting Standards, Available at: http://www.gaap.ru/biblio/icar/112000/014e.htm.

Salamon, Gerald L., and Thomas L. Stober, 1994, Cross-quarter differences in stock price responses to earnings announcements: fourth-quarter and seasonality influences, *Contemporary Accounting Research* 11, 297-330.

Salter, Stephen B., and Frederick Niswander, 1995, Cultural influence on the development of accounting systems internationally: A test of Gray's (1988) theory, *Journal of International Business Studies* 26, 379-397.

Sankar, Mandira Roy, and K.R. Subramanyam, 2001, Reporting discretion and private information communication through earnings, *Journal of Accounting Research* 39, 365-386.

Schipper, Katherine, 1989, Commentary on earnings management, *Accounting Horizons* 3, 91-102.

Schipper, Katherine, and Linda Vincent, 2003, Earnings quality, *Accounting Horizons* 17, 97-110.

Shleifer, Andrei, and Robert W. Vishny, 1997, A survey of corporate governance, *Journal of Finance* 52, 737-783.

Shleifer, Andrei and Treisman, Daniel, 2000, Without a map: Political tactics and economic reform in Russia (MIT Press, Cambridge, MA).

Scholes, Myron S., Peter G. Wilson, and Mark A. Wolfson, 1992, Firms' responses to anticipated reductions in tax rates: The tax reform act of 1986, *Journal of Accounting Research* 30, 161-185.

Scott, David W., 1992, *Multivariate density estimation: theory, practice, and visualization* (John Wiley & Sons, Inc., New York, NY).

Scott, Thomas W., 1991, Pension disclosures under SFAS No. 87: Theory and evidence, *Contemporary Accounting Research* 8, 62-81.

SEC, 2003, Report pursuant to Section 704 of the Sarbanes-Oxley Act of 2002, Available at: http://www.sec.gov/news/studies/sox704report.pdf.

Shivakumar, Lakshmanan, 1996, Estimating abnormal accruals for detection of earnings management, Working paper, Vanderbilt University.

Shivakumar, Lakshmanan, 2000, Do firms mislead investors by overstating earnings before seasoned equity offerings? *Journal of Accounting and Economics* 29, 339-371.

Skinner, Douglas J., and Richard G. Sloan, 2000, Earnings surprises, growth expectations, and stock returns or don't let an earnings torpedo sink your portfolio, *Review of Accounting Studies* 7, 289-312.

Sloan, Richard G., 1996, Do stock prices fully reflect information in accruals and cash flows about future earnings? *The Accounting Review* 71, 289-315.

Sloan, Richard G., 2001, Financial accounting and corporate governance: a discussion, *Journal of Accounting and Economics* 32, 335-347.

Smith, Clifford W., and Jerold B. Warner, 1979, On financial contracting: an analysis of bond covenants, *Journal of Financial Economics* 7, 117-161.

Strong, John S., and John R. Meyer, 1987, Asset writedowns: Managerial incentives and security returns, *Journal of Finance* 42, 643-663.

Subramanyam, K.R., 1996, The prising of discretionary accruals, *Journal of Accounting and Economics* 22, 249-281.

Sutton, Timothy G., 1988, The proposed introduction of current cost accounting in the U.K.: Determinants of corporate preference, *Journal of Accounting and Economics* 10, 127-149.

Sweeney, Amy Patricia, 1994, Debt-covenant violations and managers' accounting responses, *Journal of Accounting and Economics* 17, 281-308.

Tabor, Richard H., and James T. Willis, 1985, Empirical evidence on the changing role of analytical review procedures, *Auditing* 4, 93-109.

Teoh, Siew Hong, Ivo Welch, and T.J. Wong, 1998a, Earnings management and the underperformance of seasoned equity offerings, *Journal of Financial Economics* 50, 63-99.

Teoh, Siew Hong, Ivo Welch, and T.J. Wong, 1998b, Earnings management and the long-run market performance of initial public offerings, *The Journal of Finance* LIII, 1935-1974.

Teoh, Siew Hong, T.J. Wong, and Gita R. Rao, 1998c, Are accruals during initial public offerings opportunities? *Review of Accounting Studies* 3, 175-208.

Thomas, Jacob K., 1989, Unusual patterns in reported earnings, *The Accounting Review* 64, 773-787.

Thomas, Jacob K., and Huao-jun Zhang, 2000, Identifying unexpected accruals: a comparison of current approaches, *Journal of Accounting and Public Policy* 19, 347-376.

Wahlen, James M., 1994, The nature of information in commercial bank loan loss disclosures, *The Accounting Review* 69, 455-478.

Walking, Ralph A., and Michael S. Long, 1984, Agency theory, managerial welfare, and takeover bid resistance, *RAND Journal of Economics* 15, 54-68.

Wang, Shiing-wu, 1994, The relationship between financial reporting practices and the 1986 Alternative Minimum Tax, *Accounting Review* 69, 495-506.

Warfield, Terry D., John J. Wild, and Kenneth L. Wild, 1995, Managerial ownership, accounting choices, and informativeness of earnings, *Journal of Accounting and Economics* 20, 61-91.

Watts, Ross L., 2003a, Conservatism in accounting. Part I: Explanations and implications, *Accounting Horizons* 17, 207-221.

Watts, Ross L., 2003b, Conservatism in accounting. Part II: Evidence and research opportunities, *Accounting Horizons* 17, 287-301.

Watts, Ross L., and Jerold L. Zimmerman, 1978, Towards a positive theory of determination of accounting standards, *The Accounting Review* 53, 112-134.

Watts, Ross L., and Jerold L. Zimmerman, 1979, The demand for and supply of accounting theories: the market for excuses, *The Accounting Review* 54, 273-305.

Watts, Ross L., and Jerold L. Zimmerman, 1986, *Positive accounting theory* (Prentice-Hall, Englewood Cliffs, NJ).

Wells, Peter, 2002, Earnings management surrounding CEO change, *Accounting and Finance* 42, 169-193.

White, Halbert, 1980, A heteroskedasticity-consistent covariance matrix estimator and a direct test for heteroskedasticity, *Econometrica* 48, 817-838.

White, Halbert, 1982, Maximum likelihood estimation of misspecified models, *Econometrica* 50, 1-25.

Wiedman, Christine I., 1999, Instructional case: Detecting earnings manipulation, *Issues in Accounting Education* 14, 145-176.

Wilson, Arlette C., and Janet Colbert, 1989, An analysis of simple and rigorous decision models as analytical procedures, *Accounting Horizons* 3, 79-83.

Wong, Jilnaught, 1988, Political costs and an intraperiod accounting choice for export tax credits, *Journal of Accounting and Economics* 10, 37-51.

Xie, Biao, Wallace N. III Davidson, and Peter J. DaDalt, 2003, Earnings management ang corporate governance: the role of the board and the audit committee, *Journal of Corporate Finance* 9, 295-316.

Xie, Hong, 2001, The mispricing of abnormal accruals, *The Accounting Review* 76, 357-373.

Yakovlev, Andrei, 1998, *Neformal'nyj sektor v ekonomike Rossii: formy sushchestvovaniya, rol' i masshtaby* (ISARP, Moscow, Russia).

Zarowin, Paul, 2002, Does income smoothing make stock price more informative? Working paper, New York University.

Zimmerman, Jerold L., 1983, Taxes and firm size, *Journal of Accounting and Economics* 5, 119-149.

Zingales, Luigi, 1994, The value of the voting right: A study of the Milan stock exchange, *The Review of Financial Studies* 7, 125-148.

www.ingramcontent.com/pod-product-compliance
Ingram Content Group UK Ltd.
Pitfield, Milton Keynes, MK11 3LW, UK
UKHW020121290926
15471UKWH00003B/201

9 783631 545775